SIGHT SINGING COMPLETE

EIGHTH EDITION

Maureen Carr

Bruce Benward

with   Taylor Greer   Eric McKee   and   Phillip Torbert

SIGHT SINGING COMPLETE, EIGHTH EDITION

Published by McGraw-Hill Education, 2 Penn Plaza, New York, NY 10121. Copyright © 2015 by McGraw-Hill Education.
All rights reserved. Printed in the United States of America. Previous editions © 2007 and 1999. No part of this publication
may be reproduced or distributed in any form or by any means, or stored in a database or retrieval system, without the prior
written consent of McGraw-Hill Education, including, but not limited to, in any network or other electronic storage or
transmission, or broadcast for distance learning.

Some ancillaries, including electronic and print components, may not be available to customers outside the United States.

This book is printed on acid-free paper.

4 5 6 7 8 9 QVS/QVS 23 22 21 20 19

ISBN 978-0-07-352665-2
MHID 0-07-352665-7

Senior Vice President, Products & Markets: *Kurt L. Strand*
Vice President, General Manager, Products & Markets: *Michael Ryan*
Vice President, Content Production & Technology Services: *Kimberly Meriwether David*
Brand Manager: *Sarah Remington*
Editorial Coordinator: *Kanyakrit Vongkiatkajorn*
Marketing Manager: *Kelly Odom*
Director, Content Production: *Terri Schiesl*
Senior Content Project Manager: *Melissa M. Leick*
Buyer: *Susan K. Culbertson*
Cover Designer: *Studio Montage, St. Louis, MO.*
Cover Image: *J.S. Bach, Fuga (from Violin Sonata no. 3 in C Major, BWV 1005), notated by Joseph Joachim (1831–1907).
    Reproduced from the collections of the Library of Congress.*
Compositor: *A-R Editions, Inc.*
Typeface: 10/12 Times
Printer: *Quad/Graphics*

All credits appearing on page or at the end of the book are considered to be an extension of the copyright page.

The Internet addresses listed in the text were accurate at the time of publication. The inclusion of a website does not indicate
an endorsement by the authors or McGraw-Hill Education, and McGraw-Hill Education does not guarantee the accuracy of
the information presented at these sites.

www.mhhe.com

Contents

UNIT FIVE

UNIT SIX

UNIT FIFTEEN

UNIT SIXTEEN

Preface

Introduction

The ear tends to be lazy, craves the familiar, and is shocked by the unexpected: the eye, on the other hand, tends to be impatient, craves the novel and is bored by repetition. Thus, the average listener prefers concerts confined to works by old masters and it is only the highbrow who is willing to listen to new works, but the average reader wants the latest book and it is the classics of the past which are left to the highbrow.[1]

This passage is from an essay "Hic et Ille" (This and That) written by the modern British author, W. H. Auden. One can only imagine that if Auden were alive today, he would consider the eighth edition of Sight Singing Complete to be the remedy for the situation he is describing. In order to soften the "shock" of the "unexpected," this new edition of *Sight Singing Complete* begins with the familiar and spirals systematically to the unfamiliar. Because the ear craves the familiar, a cumulative approach is used that moves gently from the familiar toward the unexpected or unfamiliar. This strategy can be observed in three threads from the seventh edition that are woven into the tapestry of this new edition: (1) the art of the vocalise, (2) the art of improvisation, and (3) the art of reading from open score. Vocalises evolve from Models and Melodic Fragments (part B, sections 1 and 2); Improvisation from Creating Coherent Phrases part A (section 3) and part B (section 3); and Reading in Open Score from Ensemble Singing in part E. In this edition, new examples from the past nine centuries are added to supplement the existing material.

---

[1] W. H. Auden, "Hic et Ille," The Dyer's Hand and Other Essays (London: Faber and Faber, 1963), p. 100. (This essay originally appeared in April 1956 in a journal Encounter 6, no. 4.) W. H. Auden (1907–1973) served as a collaborator with Chester Kallman (1921–1975) and Igor Stravinsky (1881–1971) for The Rake's Progress (written between 1948 and 1951) after a preliminary meeting with Stravinsky in 1947.

THE ART OF THE VOCALISE

A systematic approach to vocalises begins in Unit 1 (B-1) with a stepwise pattern that descends from scale degree 5 to scale degree 1. This exercise serves as a warm-up pattern until Unit 7 (part B, section 4), where a new vocalise outlines linear harmonies of I–V7–I. As harmonic vocabulary expands, this vocalise becomes the basis for modulatory patterns that are improvisatory. In later units, art songs in the form of vocalises help to integrate the complexities of chromaticism.

THE ART OF IMPROVISATION

Working in tandem with the art of the vocalise and embellished arias is the art of improvisation. For example, in Unit 15B, section 4, the improvisation is based on rhythmic reductions of melodic frameworks from Unit 14D, section 2: Stravinsky's *Pastorale* and Rossini's *Du séjour de la lumière*. Both excerpts emphasize the same altered scale degrees (raised 4 and lowered 7). At this point in the book, students are not likely to experience "shock" with these "unexpected" alterations because of the smooth transition from the "familiar" to the "unfamiliar." By the end of the book, students are improvising in all idioms—including jazz. The capstone for Unit 13 (part B, section 4) is the exercise for students to create their own rendition on the text for "Mood Indigo." This unit also contains melodies by Duke Ellington (part D, nos. 1–6) as well as a vocalise by Alec Wilder (part C, section 2).

THE ART OF READING FROM OPEN SCORE

Ensemble singing in unfamiliar clefs, or as Auden might say "unexpected" clefs, is a necessary discipline for the complete musician. Learning to read in open score offers numerous advantages, such as strengthening intervallic reading, setting the stage for transposition, and helping students to hear orchestral scores with their "eyes." Clef reading is introduced as an exercise in ensemble singing—at first with two lines written in the soprano clef in an imitative texture. It is expected that students will become conversant with the three most common C clefs: soprano, alto, and tenor.

"Hearing music" with one's "eyes" has served as the purpose of *Sight Singing Complete* since the first edition in 1965. In order to reach this goal, the sequence of events is designed to help students develop the aural skills that will enable them to reverse the compositional process of sound into symbol to one of symbol into sound. Just as painters speak of the "thinking eye" (Klee), playwrights and poets of the "mind's eye" (Shakespeare), and psychologists of the "soul's eye," musicians are trained to develop a "hearing eye." For only when students are able to translate musical symbols from the concrete level of musical notation into sounds will they be able to approximate the abstract musical ideas that the composer was trying to communicate in the first place. The task of observing a musical score with thoughtful and hearing eyes is the most significant outcome of the four-semester sequence of courses for which this textbook is designed.

The idea of replaying a work of art in one's mind is not unique to music. For example, a scholar of Elizabethan drama encourages the reader of a play by Shakespeare "to rehearse the play in his [or her] mind, considering the text in detail as an actor would, hearing and seeing each moment."[2] The student of music has precisely the same goal: to be able to rehearse the musical score in his or her mind, considering the musical notation in detail as a conductor, performer, or composer would—hearing and seeing each moment.

Helpful Strategies

Sight singing is one of the most practical means that students have of demonstrating to their instructors the progress they are making in "hearing" the notation they are "seeing." For this reason, various strategies exist to help students improve their aural skills.

1. **Syllables or numbers.** Learn thoroughly whatever syllable or numbering system your instructor recommends. To take the guesswork out of sight singing, it is important to "know" the scale degree of all melody notes and to communicate that information to your instructor—as well as to yourself.

2. **Intervals.** Knowing what E sounds like when you are presently singing C is something to get accustomed to. At first it may be difficult, but when you

learn that from C to E is the same distance as from F to A or G to B, your problem is diminished considerably. Learning to sing intervals (distance between pitches) is an absolute must.

3. **Familiarity with the scale.** Figure out the key of each melody and sing the scale before attacking the melody itself.

4. **Reference tones.** Isolate the 1st, 3rd, and 5th scale degrees and sing them until memorized. Then, for a while at least, circle all 1st, 3rd, and 5th scale degrees in the melody. These are called reference tones.

5. **The tonic note.** You should be able to pause anywhere in a melody and sing the tonic (1st scale degree) pitch immediately. Try it a few times just to make sure you can do it.

6. **"Hearing" what you are "seeing."** Practice scanning melodies—thinking (rather than singing) what each pitch sounds like. The sooner you can do this, the closer you will be to developing a "hearing eye."

7. **Steady tempo.** Avoid starts and stops in sight singing. Doing so means that the tempo you selected may be too fast—your voice gets ahead of your mind.

8. **Rhythm.** Trying to figure out the next pitch and rhythm at the same time may be overwhelming at first. Before singing, tap out the rhythm of the entire melody. This "divide and conquer" technique will help considerably, and you will soon be able to coordinate both.

New to the Eighth Edition

The 8th edition of *Sight Singing Complete* preserves the multi-faceted pedagogical approach and the commitment to historical repertoire from the seventh edition. New to this edition is an integrated approach to rhythm and performance—the ultimate goal being to deepen the student's musicality through a principle of physical embodiment. When a student sings one line in a musical texture, plays another line, and then sings and plays both lines together, the result is a more physical and enriching musical experience. Our approach to musicianship integrates aspects of three different skills into a single activity that combines sight singing, score reading, and rhythmic fluency. At present there are many manuals and textbooks that teach each of these skills in isolation. This edition is unusual in that we not only expect students to master each skill by itself, we also expect them to integrate all three skills in a carefully designed sequence of "Play + Sing" exercises adapted from 18th–21st-century instrumental and vocal repertoire. In each chapter, the

---

[2] Robert Hapgood, "Shakespeare and the Included Spectator" (commentary on John Russell Brown, "Laughter in the Last Plays," Shakespeare's Plays in Performance [London, 1967] In Reinterpretations of Elizabethan Drama, edited by Norman Rabkin, p. 133. New York: Columbia University Press, 1969). The essay was also cited in Michael Cohen, Hamlet in My Mind's Eye. Athens and London: University of Georgia Press, 1989.

Play + Sing section focuses on a different rhythmic challenge with each unit building on the skills achieved in previous exercises.

For example, in Unit 8 students are expected to become fluent in playing and singing excerpts from simplified versions of 19th-century waltzes. The rhythmic challenge is hemiolic melodies in $\frac{3}{2}$ meter that sound against a standard oom-pah-pah accompaniment in $\frac{3}{4}$—in short, polymeter. In Unit 10, we introduce hemiolic melodies whose downbeats are shifted to beat 2 of the notated meter, resulting in non-aligned downbeats between the melody and the accompaniment. Then, for one of the culminating "Play + Sing" exercises in Unit 16, we expect students to perform an excerpt from Stravinsky's ballet *Petrushka*. In this excerpt Stravinsky quotes a waltz theme by Joseph Lanner, which itself contains a hemiolic melody. Juxtaposed simultaneously against the waltz is the Moor's music—a simple modal melody set in $\frac{2}{4}$. Thus, this passage combines three musical strands in three different meters. The gradual progression and sequencing of skills among these three exercises ultimately leads to greater rhythmic fluency. It is one thing for students to *hear* two different levels of rhythm and meter in a musical passage; this is a challenging but essentially passive musical activity. It is another thing altogether for them to *perform* the different rhythmic and metric levels in that passage at the same time. The overall goal of the Play + Sing exercises is to cultivate musicians who are well-rounded, creative, and independent.

There are three additional advantages of the regimen of Play + Sing exercises in this edition. The first is the wide range of repertoire included in the group as a whole—from British fiddle tunes and Bizet operas to a classic hit by Dave Brubeck. The second is harmony and voice-leading. By providing a fuller musical texture, we are also providing a harmonic context for a given melodic fragment, which allows the instructor the opportunity for a more holistic approach, potentially bringing together concepts from written theory and aural skills. The previous edition had already established a link between the conceptual world of the typical theory curriculum and the aural skills classroom; the eighth edition enhances this pedagogical bridge. The third is flexibility. Since some arrangements include 3 or 4 lines, there is the potential for a student or group of students to focus on different combinations of voices in both solo and ensemble settings.

Summary of New Features

1. A more comprehensive approach to rhythmic studies including units on 3 against 2, hemiola, 4 against 3, irregular/additive meter, and polymeter.

2. Play + Sing exercises in all sixteen units spanning Bach to Brubeck.

3. Melodic excerpts from a wide range of sources, including various folk songs from different regions of the world, choral repertoire, and symphonic works.

Format of the Text

The text is divided into sixteen units, and, except for the last unit, in which parts C and D are merged, each contains five parts: A, B, C, D, E. Each part constitutes a track, or procedure, that is developed throughout all sixteen units.

A: RHYTHM

Most units begin with rhythm modules that are then combined into phrases. Students are asked to create coherent phrases from the modules that they have just learned. Although rhythm syllables are not provided in this edition, it is strongly recommended that a system be adopted. Conducting patterns are by Dennis Glocke, Director of Concert Bands at the Penn State School of Music.

B: MODELS AND MELODIC FRAGMENTS FOR INTERVAL SINGING

This part aims to provide students with melodic patterns derived from music literature. Initially, the focus is on hearing and singing before reading, so that students will become familiar with melodic patterns aurally before they are asked to read them in notation. The process of melodic fragmentation serves a number of purposes. The brevity of each fragment (at least in the earlier units) allows students to focus on the specific musical element or elements of the given harmonies. Of necessity, the melodic fragments in the later units become longer than those of the earlier ones because the "vocabulary" is more complicated in chromatic and atonal structures. In section 3 of part B, students are asked to create coherent melodies on the basis of the melodic fragments they have just learned. (To give students the experience of reading through as many of the key signatures represented in the circle of 5ths as possible, an attempt is made to systematically introduce new key signatures.) In section 4 of part B, students are introduced to the art of improvisation; vocalise exercises are incorporated into this section in units 7–12.

C: SHORTER AND EASIER MELODIES TO BE SUNG AT PERFORMANCE TEMPO

This part provides an opportunity for students to test their sight singing skills for continuity, accuracy, and musicality. These melodies are shorter, contain few problem intervals or rhythms, require little or no preparation, and are intended to be sung at sight on the first attempt.

D: MELODIES FOR MORE COMPREHENSIVE STUDY

Part D of units 1–14 are made up entirely of tonal melodies, lending themselves quite appropriately to solfeggio, or number systems. Because the materials in units 15 and 16 are more contemporary, systems such as "neutral syllable," chromatic fixed-Do, or integers 0–11 are more appropriate. (Notice that in Unit 16, sections C and D are merged.)

E: ENSEMBLES AND PLAY + SING

The repertoire for ensemble singing is expanded in this edition to provide students with appropriate experiences for score reading with C clefs as well as treble and bass clefs. A new pedagogical thread appears in part E of all units called Play + Sing exercises to develop musical fluency in two dimensions: singing one line and playing another at the keyboard.

The Available Systems

Most instructors who have taught sight singing for years have either chosen or developed a system with which they feel comfortable. Those who are teaching the course for the first time may be interested in the variety of approaches that are available:

Moveable Do. In one "moveable do" system, the tonic pitch is do in major and minor keys; in the other system, the tonic pitch of minor keys is represented by la.

Fixed Do. Do is always the same note (usually C) regardless of the key. One "fixed do" system uses only seven syllables regardless of chromatic changes; in the other system, chromatic changes are accounted for (chromatic "fixed do").

Moveable Numbers. Similar in design to moveable do, numbers (most often 1–7) are substituted for the solfeggio syllables. The tonic note becomes "1."

Fixed Numbers. A system similar to chromatic fixed do, "0" is always the same pitch class (usually C).

SOME MOVEABLE AND FIXED SYSTEMS IN MAJOR KEYS

G-Major Scale	G	A	B	C	D	E	F♯	G
Seven-syllable moveable Do	Do	Re	Mi	Fa	Sol	La	Ti	Do
Seven-syllable fixed Do	Sol	La	Ti	Do	Re	Mi	Fa	Sol
Seven-number moveable system	1	2	3	4	5	6	7	1

SOME MOVEABLE SYSTEMS FOR MINOR KEYS

G-Harmonic Minor Scale	G	A	B♭	C	D	E♭	F♯	G
La-based minor	La	Ti	Do	Re	Mi	Fa	Si	La
Do-based minor	Do	Re	Me	Fa	Sol	Le	Ti	Do
One-based minor	1	2	3	4	5	6	7	1

TWELVE-SYLLABLE OR NUMBER SYSTEMS

The use of 12 symbols makes possible a label for all pitch classes of the octave. Some examples are:

G-Major Scale	G	(G♯)	A	(A♯)	B	C	(C♯)	D	(D♯)	E	(E♯)	F♯
Twelve-tone fixed Do	†Sol	Si	La	Li	Ti	Do	Di	Re	Ri	Mi	Mis	Fi
Twelve-tone fixed numbers	7	8	9	10	11	0	1	2	3	4	5	6

---

†Descending order is: Sol Se Fa Mi Me Re Ra Do Ti Te La Le Sol

Acknowledgments

IN MEMORIAM

BRUCE BENWARD (1921–2007)

"A teacher affects eternity;
he can never tell where his influence stops."

—Henry Adams.
The Education of Henry Adams (1907), 20

Bruce Benward's arrival at the University of Wisconsin-Madison in 1965 coincided with the first edition of *Sight Singing Complete (SSC)*, one of a long series of important and influential textbooks in sight singing, ear training, and music theory.

With this 8th edition (2015) of *SSC*, we celebrate both the 50th anniversary of the first edition and Bruce Benward's distinguished career as a master teacher who devoted his energies to passing the art and craft of teaching to his students. We also acknowledge the generosity of his spirit and that of his wife Gene (1923–2004), who was a partner in assisting with the musical examples in the early editions.

Bruce was a valued mentor during my graduate student days at the University of Wisconsin–Madison (that began in 1966), and I am immensely grateful to him for our pedagogical collaborations for the 5th, 6th, and 7th editions of *SSC*. With the 8th edition, I am delighted to have enlisted the gracious assistance of three of my colleagues from The Pennsylvania State University: Taylor Greer, Eric McKee, and Phillip Torbert. The four of us are equal partners in this endeavor of moving the book forward. Bruce's legacy of positive energy, mutual respect and admiration was ever-present in our meetings; his spirit lives on in this 50th anniversary edition of *SSC*.

This edition benefitted from the thoughtful reviews written by William Marvin of the Eastman School of Music and David Patterson of the University of Massachusetts, Boston. Phillip Torbert is responsible for the cover concept.

Kevin LaVine of the Library of Congress helped us to secure the cover image of J.S. Bach, Fuga (from Violin Sonata no. 3 in C Major, BWV 1005), notated by Joseph Joachim (1831–1907).

I also wish to thank the editors for the extraordinary care with which they treated us and our manuscript: Sarah Remington, sponsoring editor; Kanyakrit Vongkiatkajorn, developmental editor; Anne Wallingford and Janet Woods, permissions coordinators; Melissa Leick, project manager; and James L. Zychowicz and Bonnie Balke of A-R Editions, responsible for the encoding of the music notation. Each level of the process that resulted in the publication of this edition was characterized by professionalism, humanism, and optimism.

Maureen Carr

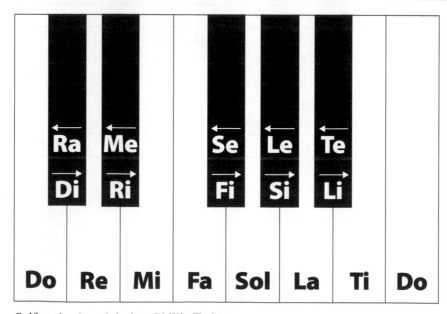

Solfege keyboard design: Phillip Torbert

UNIT ONE

A Rhythm—Simple Meter: One-, Two-, Three-, and Four-Beat Values and Duple Division of the Beat

SECTION 1. Modules in Simple Meter

Using a neutral syllable, sing the patterns in each of the given modules. Begin by repeating each module several times. Then treat the successive modules as a continuous exercise.

Notice that the values of the notes and rests in these modules encompass one, two, three, or four beats. The quarter note represents the beat in meters such as $[\frac{2}{4}]$, $[\frac{3}{4}]$, and $[\frac{4}{4}]$; the eighth note in $[\frac{3}{8}]$ and $[\frac{4}{8}]$; the sixteenth note in $[\frac{4}{16}]$; the half note in $[\frac{4}{2}]$; the whole note in $[\frac{3}{1}]$; and so on. In subsequent chapters you will learn how to divide beats. This process will help you understand the difference between simple and compound meter.

Use the conducting patterns shown below, if your instructor recommends you do so.

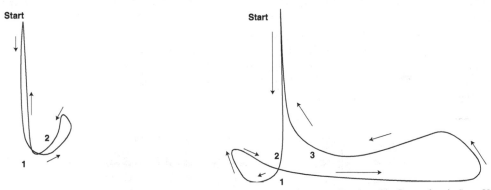

Credit: All conducting patterns in this edition are designed by Dennis Glocke, Director of Concert Bands at The Pennsylvania State University School of Music.

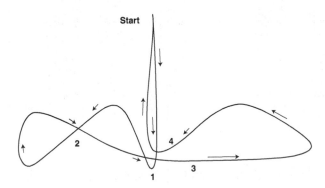

1.
Rhythm:
2.
3.
4.
5.
6.
7.
8.
9.
10.
11.
12.
13.
14.
15.
16.
17.
18.
19.
20.
21.
22.
23.
24.
25.
26.
27.
28.
29.
30.
31.
32.
33.
34.
35.
36.
37.
38.
39.
40.
41.
42.
43.
44.
45.
46.
47.
48.
49.

SECTION 2. Phrases in Simple Meter

Eventually, you will learn to internalize the beat, but in the early stages of learning to read rhythms you can use a number of procedures:

1. Clap the meter and sing the rhythm (use a neutral syllable or the system of rhythm syllables recommended by your instructor).
2. Sing the meter and clap the rhythm.
3. Tap the meter with one hand and the rhythm with the other.
4. Half the class taps the meter while the other half claps the rhythm.

SECTION 3. Creating a Coherent Phrase in Simple Meter

Choose one of the simple meters found in section 1. Using rhythmic patterns provided in section 1, create a coherent four-measure phrase.

Write your solution on the following line:

B Diatonic Models and Melodic Fragments: M2 and m2

SECTION 1. Diatonic Models

(A) VOCALISE DESCENDING FROM $\hat{5}$ TO $\hat{1}$

Neighboring tone figures in combination with passing tone figures outline a descending line from scale degrees 5 to 1. Exercises 1–3 combine neighboring and passing tone figures to fill in a descending line from scale degrees 5 to 1 in major and minor. These passages (or *vocalises*) may be used as a way to establish the key for tonal exercises and melodies throughout the book.

Procedure

MODELS 1–3

Step 1. Your instructor sings or plays figure 1 (major) as a means of establishing the key.

Step 2. Repeat (sing) the same figure your instructor provides in step 1.

Step 3. For additional practice, follow the same procedure in each major key by moving down a perfect 5th (or up a perfect 4th), first to F major, then to B♭, E♭, and so on. See the following model:

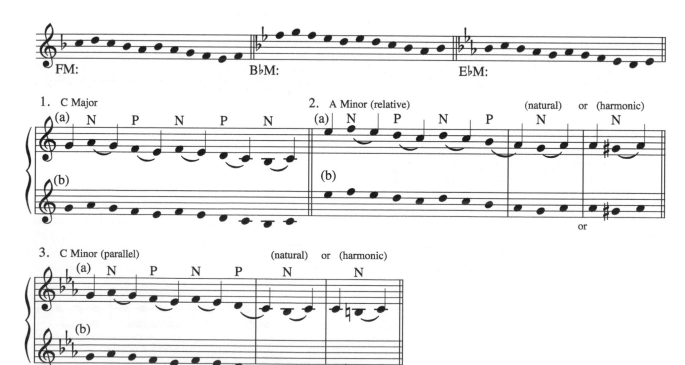

(B) VOCALISE DESCENDING FROM $\hat{1}$ TO $\hat{5}$ AND ASCENDING FROM $\hat{5}$ TO $\hat{1}$

Double neighboring tone figures at cadential points will help you confirm the tonic of a key. This model will be useful to you in writing creative exercises. As with the previous vocalise, this passage may be used as a way to establish the key for tonal exercises and melodies throughout the book.

Procedure

MODEL 4

Follow the same procedure for singing this vocalise in different keys down a 5th (or up a 4th).

FM: B♭M: E♭M:

4. C Major

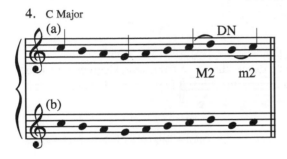

(a)   DN

M2   m2

(b)

(C) VOCALISE ASCENDING FROM $\hat{1}$ TO $\hat{5}$ AND DESCENDING FROM $\hat{5}$ TO $\hat{1}$

Procedure

MODEL 5

Follow the same procedure for singing this vocalise in different keys down a 5th (or up a 4th).

FM: B♭M: E♭M:

5. C Major

(a)

(b)

SECTION 2. Melodic Fragments in F Major

These melodic fragments are taken from music literature for the purpose of providing a musical context for the intervals M2 and m2. Examples of neighboring, passing, and double neighboring tones occur in abundance.

Procedure

1. Your instructor establishes the key for each of the fragments, using one of the *vocalises* taught in exercises 1, 2, 3, 4, or 5 transposed to the appropriate pitch level.

2. Sing the following excerpts and identify neighboring, passing, and double neighboring tone figures as well as intervals.

1. *Kyrie eleison*—Lord Have Mercy—Requiem Mass.   Gregorian Chant
♩ = 144

2. *Veni Sancte Spiritus*—Come Holy Spirit—Pentecost (abridged).   Gregorian Chant
♩ = 144

3. *hôdu*—Praise—Passover.   Adapted from Idelsohn collection *Gesänge der Babylonischen Juden*—Songs of the Babylonian Jews, #23
♩ = 144

4. *im afès*—Selihot—Forgiveness (a specific series of blessings).   Adapted from Idelsohn collection: *Gesänge der Babylonischen Juden* —Songs of the Babylonian Jews, #43
♩ = 144

5. The Coulin (lament).   Adapted from a Gaelic lament
♩ = 144

6. Orlando di Lasso   "Beati quorum remissae sunt" (Blessed is he whose transgressions are forgiven), measures 19–23
♩ = 60

Adapted from "Psalmus Secundus Poenitentialis" ["Beati quorum remissae sunt iniquitates"] by Orlando di Lasso, and published in *Orlando di Lasso: The Seven Penitential Psalms and Laudate Dominum de caelis,* edited by Peter Bergquist. Recent Researches in the Music of the Renaissance, vols. 86–87. Madison, Wisconsin: A-R Editions, Inc. 1990. Used with permission.

7.

Orlando di Lasso "Domine, ne in furore" (Oh Lord do not rebuke me), measures 33–39

Adapted from "Psalmus Primus Poenitentialis" ["Domine, ne in furore tuo"] by Orlando di Lasso, and published in *Orlando di Lasso: The Seven Penitential Psalms and Laudate Dominum de caelis,* edited by Peter Bergquist. Recent Researches in the Music of the Renaissance, vols. 86–87. Madison, Wisconsin: A-R Editions, Inc. 1990. Used with permission.

Adapted from a song by Charles E. Graaf, composed in the Hague, 1766; the basis for Mozart's Eight Variations, K. Anh. 208 (24), meas. 1–4.

8.

Adapted from "Ah, vous dirai-je, Maman" (Ah! I will Tell You, Mama) composed in Paris, 1778; the basis for Mozart's Twelve Variations, K. 265(300e), meas. 1–8.

9.

10.

Johann Pachelbel Chorale 64, *Wenn wir in höchsten Nöten sein* (When We Are in Utmost Need), meas. 22–25 (transposed)

SECTION 3. Creating a Coherent Melody

Return to section 2 and select two or three segments of melodic fragments 1–5. Place them in an order that would create a coherent chant. Here is an example based on the first and last segments of fragment 4 and the first segment of fragment 5.

SECTION 4. Improvisation

The best way to learn the "art of improvisation" is to restrict yourself to the metric and melodic patterns that you have already experienced in unit 1.

Here are some guidelines to ensure a logical outcome:

1. Establish a rhythmic framework (and/or)
2. Establish a tonal outline

For example:

1. Rhythmic framework:

2. Tonal outline:

3. Possible outcome:

C Melodies by Bruce Benward (Major): M2 and m2

1. Establish the key for each of the following melodies by singing one of the *vocalises* presented earlier.
2. Using syllables or numbers, sing the melody.
3. Try to differentiate between neighboring and passing tone figures as you read each melody.

1. Scale: C Major

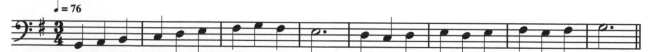

2. Scale: G Major

3. Scale: F Major

4. Scale: D Major

5. Scale: B-flat Major

6. Scale: A Major

7. Scale: E-flat Major

8. Scale: E Major

9. Scale: A-flat Major

10. Scale: B Major

11. Scale: C Major
Moderato

12. Scale: G Major
Allegro

13. Scale: F Major
Allegro

14. Scale: B-flat Major

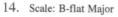

15. Scale: D Major

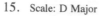

The last four measures of number 16 are in contrary motion to the first four.

16. Scale: E-flat Major

17. Scale: A Major

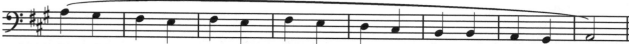

18. Scale: A-flat Major

19. Scale: E Major

20. Scale: C Major

Allegro

p

D Melodies

SECTION 1. Melodies by Bruce Benward (Major): P5, P4, M3, and m3 within the Tonic Triad and M2 and m2

1. Establish the key for each of the following melodies by singing a *vocalise*.
2. Using syllables or numbers, sing the melody.
3. Try to consider the elements of the triad as *reference tones*.

SECTION 2. Russian Folksongs: P5, P4, M3, m3, M2, and m2 within the Diatonic Scale

Pyotr Tchaikovsky "My Green Vineyard"

2. **Not quickly**   Tchaikovsky   "On the Green Meadow" (transposed)

3. **Quickly**   Tchaikovsky   "Play My Bagpipes" (transposed)

4. Moderately

Tchaikovsky "Like a Princess in the Town" (melody transposed)

5. Allegro vivo

Mily Balakirev A Collection of Popular Russian Songs, no. 25 "Round Dance"
(subtitled "From the Tambov Governate")

6. Allegro con brio

Balakirev A Collection of Popular Russian Songs, no. 26 "Round Dance"
(subtitled "From the Nizhny Novgorod Governate, Arzamas County")

E Ensembles and Play + Sing

SECTION 1. Repertoire Using Treble and Bass Clefs

This two-voice section is intended to provide practice in ensemble singing in familiar clefs (treble and bass). The melody lines are similar to those found in part C of this unit, but now you must learn to think in two melodic dimensions. For individual practice, you could sing one line and play the other line at the keyboard. This would be excellent preparation for the classroom experience of singing in ensemble.

Follow the procedures outlined in part C for establishing the key.

SECTION 2. Repertoire Using C Clefs

This two-voice section is intended to provide practice in ensemble singing in unfamiliar clefs (soprano, alto and tenor clefs). The placement of the clef on the staff indicates middle C. The soprano clef places middle C on the bottom line; the alto clef places middle C on the middle line; the tenor clef places middle C on the second line from the top.

The following excerpt will appear in all three clefs in this first unit to demonstrate how fluency in clef reading helps to build the skills required for the art of transposing from one key to another.

1. Both voices of the first excerpt are in the soprano clef. The starting note is G (key of C major).
2. Both voices of the second excerpt are in the alto clef. The starting note is C (key of F major).
3. Both voices of the third excerpt are in the tenor clef. The starting note is A (key of D major).

Johann Joseph Fux #17 of Serie VII—Theoretische und pädigogische Werke from *Samtliche Werke* (Theoretical and Pedagogical Works, vol. VII of the Complete Works)

1.

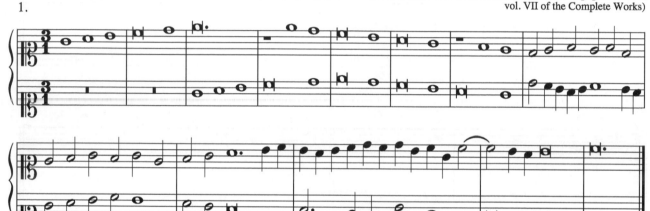

Reprinted by permission of Akademische Druck u. Verlagsanstalt, Graz, Austria.

Johann Joseph Fux #17 of Serie VII—Theoretische und pädigogische Werke from *Samtliche Werke* (Theoretical and Pedagogical Works, vol. VII of the Complete Works)

2.

Reprinted by permission of Akademische Druck u. Verlagsanstalt, Graz, Austria.

3.

Reprinted by permission of Akademische Druck u. Verlagsanstalt, Graz, Austria.

SECTION 3. Play + Sing

Johann Sebastian Bach *Jesu, meines Glaubens Zier* (Jesus, Ornament of My Faith), BWV 472, meas. 1–2

1.

Bach *Mein Jesu, dem die Seraphinen* (My Jesus, Whom the Seraphim Serve), BWV 486, meas. 1–2

2.

UNIT TWO

A   Rhythm—Compound Meter

SECTION 1.   Modules in Compound Meter

Using a neutral syllable, sing each of the given modules. Begin by repeating each module several times. Then treat the successive modules as a continuous exercise.

Notice that each beat in these modules is divisible by three. This triple division of the beat allows us to determine whether these modules are in compound meter as opposed to simple meter. Each beat in the compound meter of [$\frac{6}{8}$] is a dotted quarter note. Therefore, in [$\frac{6}{8}$] there are two beats, each divisible by three; in [$\frac{9}{8}$] three beats, each divisible by three; in [$\frac{12}{8}$] four beats, each divisible by three, and so on. Each beat in the compound meter of [$\frac{6}{4}$] is a dotted half note. Therefore, in [$\frac{6}{4}$] there are two beats, each divisible by three, and so on.

Use the conducting pattern shown below if your instructor recommends you do so.

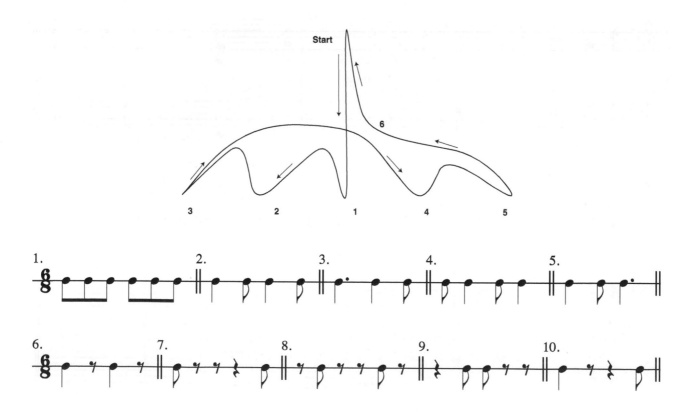

SECTION 2. Phrases in Compound Meter

For numbers 1–5, follow the procedures outlined in unit 1A, section 2. For the two-part exercises (6–9), the instructor should assign students to each part. Students should also be encouraged to practice these two-part exercises individually, using the left hand for tapping out the lower part and the right hand the upper part.

1.

2.

3.

4.

5.

6. Rhythmic ostinato plus rhythmic imitation

7. Rhythmic alternation (examples also of rhythmic hocket)

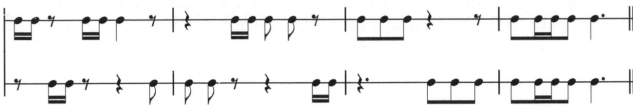

8. Rhythmic imitation

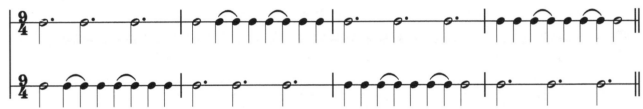

9. Rhythmic imitation

SECTION 3. Creating a Coherent Phrase in Compound Meter

Choose one of the compound meters found in section 1. Using rhythmic patterns provided in section 1, create a coherent four-measure phrase.

Write your solution on the following staff (or staves, in case you decide to write a two-voice composition):

B   Diatonic Models and Melodic Fragments: P5, P4, M3, m3, M2, and m2

SECTION 1.   Diatonic Models

These models anticipate the melodic fragments in the next section.

(A) INTERVALS OF THE 3rd OUTLINING P5s IN MAJOR KEYS

Use a G-major vocalise as a warm-up. Sing this exercise as written (in G major), and then transpose the entire set down a P5 to the key of C major. Continue the process through the keys of F, B♭, E♭, and so on.

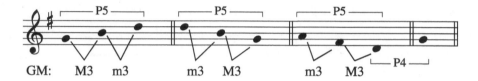

(B) PASSING TONE FIGURES IN MINOR FILLING IN 3rds

Follow the same procedure for passing tone figures in major keys. Use a vocalise in G minor (parallel minor).

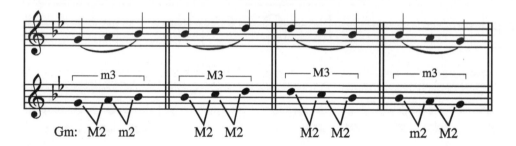

(C) INTERVALS OF THE P4, P5, AND M3 SUPPORTING A MELODIC ASCENT FROM $\hat{1}$–$\hat{3}$

Use a G major vocalise as a warm-up. After singing the intervals that outline scale degrees 1–3, sing the entire pattern in different keys as shown in the model:

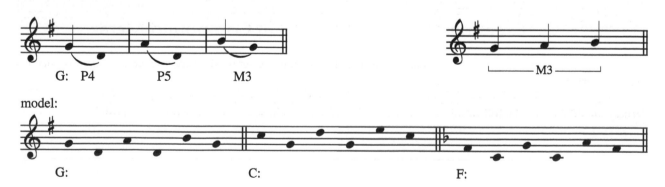

model:

SECTION 2. Melodic Fragments in G Major and G Minor

These melodic fragments are taken from music literature for the purpose of providing a musical context for the intervals introduced in the previous section.

Follow the procedure outlined in unit 1B, section 2.

1. Bach   Chorale Cantata 26, *Ach wie nichtig, ach wie flüchtig* (Ah, How Empty! Ah, How Fleeting!) (transposed)

2. Bach   Chorale, *Brunnquell aller Güter* (Fount [source] of All Goodness), BWV 445, meas. 1–6 (original key)

3. Bach   Chorale, *Jesu, deine Liebeswunden* (Jesus, Your Wounds of Love), BWV 471, phrases 1 and 4 (transposed)

4. Mozart   German Dance no. 5, K. 509 (transposed)

5. Mozart   *Sanctus* from *Requiem*, K. 626, (transposed)

6. Mozart   Eight Variations, K. 613, Variation 8 (transposed), meas. 1–4

7. Mozart   Theme and Two Variations, K. 460 (454a) Theme (transposed and adapted), meas. 1–8

Mozart "La belle Françoise" composed in Paris, 1778; the basis for Mozart's 12 Variations, K. 353 (300f), (transposed) meas. 1–4 (top line)

8.

Mozart "La belle Françoise" composed in Paris, 1778; the basis for Mozart's 12 Variations, K. 353 (300f), (transposed) meas. 1–4 (middle line)

9.

Mozart "La belle Françoise" composed in Paris, 1778; the basis for Mozart's 12 Variations, K. 353 (300f), (transposed) meas. 1–4 (bottom line)

10.

All three lines (8, 9, 10) should be combined in ensemble.

SECTION 3. Creating a Coherent Melody

Return to section 2 and select two or three segments of melodic fragments that create a coherent melody. It may be necessary to change the meter and rhythm of certain segments, depending on your choices. Here is an example based on measures 1 and 2 of fragment 1 and measures 2 and 3 of fragment 4.

SECTION 4. Improvisation

1. Take melodic fragment 10* as the basis for improvising an upper voice.

*Mozart. "La belle Françoise" composed in Paris, 1778; the basis for Mozart's 12 Variations K. 353 (300 f), (transposed) meas. 1–4 (bottom line)

2. Use the upper voice that you have created and improvise a new bass line. (For inspiration you might want to study the 12 Variations K. 353 (300 f) that Mozart composed on this tune.)

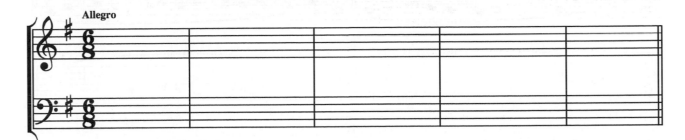

C Melodies (Major): P5, P4, M3, and m3 within the Tonic Triad and M2, and m2

The melodic content of this section focuses on some leaps within the tonic triad (M3, m3, P5, P4) as well as stepwise motion (M2 and m2) in C major.

These drills, although valuable for review and practice in singing at performance tempo, are suitable also for developing the art of clef reading as a means of transposing from one key to another. For example, the same phrase is used in both number 1 and number 11, except that in number 11 the alto clef is introduced. This places middle C (c') on the middle line. The alto clef in number 11 makes it possible to transpose number 1 to the key of D major without changing the position of any of the notes on the staff.

Procedure

1. In your mind, replace the treble clef in number 2 with an alto clef (see number 11 to visualize an alto clef).
2. Because all melodies in this section are in C major, you know that number 2 begins on the dominant (5, or Sol).
3. When you visualize number 2 with an alto clef, the first pitch is A (below middle C). A is now the dominant (5, or sol) and D is the tonic of the melody.
4. Imagine two sharps (F♯ and C♯) in the signature and sing the melody the same way as you sing it in C major with a treble clef.
5. If you sing the melody in the alto clef, it will be a 7th lower than in treble, but most melodies in this book are intended to be sung in whatever range the singer finds most comfortable.
6. If you have trouble reading in the alto clef, check your accuracy by going back to C major with a treble clef and singing the melody again.
7. Your unfamiliarity with this new clef will disappear presently, and you will have learned a valuable new skill that you may use many times later on.

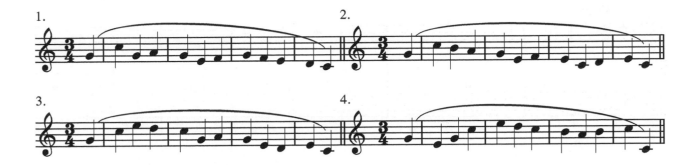

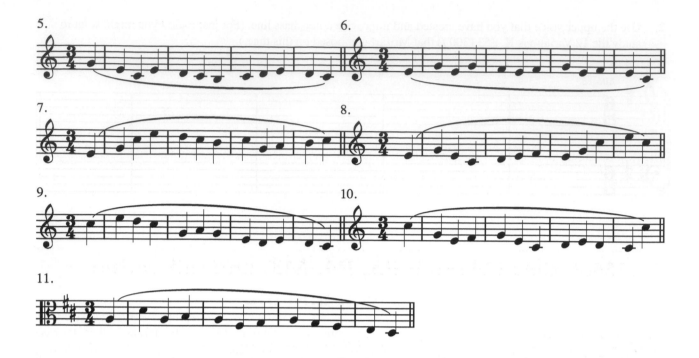

D Melodies (Major): P5, P4, M3, m3, M2, and m2 within the Diatonic Scale

SECTION 1. Excerpts from Beethoven and Haydn

The following melodies excerpted from music literature illustrate the same intervals presented in part C of this unit.

Numbers 1–10 are from Beethoven's symphonic works, and 11–20 are from Haydn's keyboard compositions. For the purposes of this unit, some of the Haydn melodies have been slightly altered or abridged. The authors of this book adjusted the melodies to ensure a comfortable singing range and to stay within the rhythmic and melodic limitations imposed by the materials of the first two units. However, those excerpts from Beethoven symphonies are the original version.

Sing these melodies using whatever procedures your instructor requests.

SECTION 2. Scottish Tunes

"The Glen of Copsewood" (adapted)

1.
Slow and Pointedly

From *The Airs and Melodies Peculiar to the Highlands of Scotland and the Isles*.
Edited by Captain Simon Fraser (Inverness: Hugh Mackenzie, 1874)

2.   "How Can We Abstain from Whisky" (adapted)

From *The Airs and Melodies Peculiar to the Highlands of Scotland and the Isles.*
Edited by Captain Simon Fraser (Inverness: Hugh Mackenzie, 1874)

3.   "The Highland Troop" (adapted)

From *The Airs and Melodies Peculiar to the Highlands of Scotland and the Isles.*
Edited by Captain Simon Fraser (Inverness: Hugh Mackenzie, 1874)

4.

From *The Airs and Melodies Peculiar to the Highlands of Scotland and the Isles*.
Edited by Captain Simon Fraser (Inverness: Hugh Mackenzie, 1874)

5.   "Niel Gow's Lament for His Second Wife" (adapted)

Slow and Pathetick

From *Collection of Strathspey's Reels & c* (Edinburgh: Rob Purdie, 1809)

6.   "The Irish Washerwoman"

(Boston: Oliver Ditson, 1856)

E Ensembles and Play + Sing

SECTION 1. Repertoire Using Treble and Bass Clefs

The first three ensemble excerpts are from Beethoven's *Missa Solemnis,* op. 123: (1) Gloria, (2) Credo, and (3) Benedictus. Each melodic line operates within the same intervallic restrictions of this unit. The fourth excerpt, by Orlando di Lasso, provides another setting of the Benedictus written much earlier than the Beethoven.

Because each excerpt is imitative, sing each line as a separate melodic exercise before you try to put the two together. The texts from Gloria, Credo, and Benedictus are provided, although you need not use words in performing these.

---

* See section A of this unit for compound meter.

  As a warm-up for ensemble singing, each line should be performed as a solo exercise.

  When the students are ready to sing in ensemble, the instructor should provide the first few notes of each part at entrances, either by singing with the students or by articulating these patterns at the keyboard.

4.

Be - ne - di - ctus, _____ qui ve -

Be - ne - di - ctus, _____ qui

- nit in no - mi - ne _____ Do -

ve - nit in no - mi - ne Do -

- mi - ni, in no - mi - ne, _____ in no - mi - ne, _____

- mi - ni, in no - mi - ne, _____ in no - mi - ne, _____

_ in no - mi - ne _____ Do - mi - ni.

_ in no - mi - ne _____ Do - mi - ni.

New York: Appleton-Century-Crofts, Inc.—G. Soderlund

SECTION 2. Repertoire Using C Clefs

Johann Joseph Fux   #27 of Serie VII—Theoretische und pädigogische Werke from *Samtliche Werke* (Theoretical and Pedagogical Works, vol. VII of the Complete Works)

1.

Reprinted by permission of Akademische Druck u. Verlagsanstalt, Graz, Austria.

Johann Joseph Fux   #28 of Serie VII—Theoretische und pädigogische Werke from *Samtliche Werke* (Theoretical and Pedagogical Works, vol. VII of the Complete Works)

2.

Reprinted by permission of Akademische Druck u. Verlagsanstalt, Graz, Austria.

SECTION 3. Play + Sing

1.

Bach   *Wo ist mein Schäflein, das ich liebe* (Where Is My Lamb Which I Love), BWV 507

2.

Bach   *Liebes Herz, bedenke doch* (Dear Heart, Consider Yet), BWV 482

UNIT THREE

A Rhythm—Simple Meter: Further Duple Division of the Beat

SECTION 1. Modules in Simple Meter

Using rhythm syllables or a neutral syllable, sing each of the given modules. Begin by repeating each module several times. Then treat the successive modules as a continuous exercise.

Notice that each beat in these modules is divisible by two. This duple division of the beat allows you to determine whether these modules are in simple meter or compound meter. Each beat in the simple meter of [$\frac{4}{4}$] is a quarter note. Therefore, in [$\frac{4}{4}$] there are four beats, each divisible by two; in [$\frac{3}{4}$] three beats, each divisible by two; and so on.

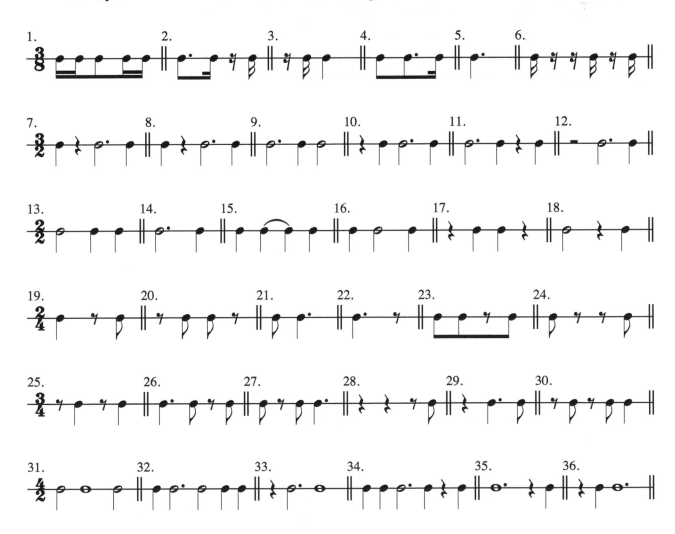

Calypso patterns related to song 5 in part C, section 2, of this unit.

Calypso patterns related to "Banana Boat Song" (see unit 3C2, example 3)

Syncopation patterns from Stravinsky's Octet for Wind Instruments, R-73:1–4 with the rests omitted. (see unit 3C2, example 4)

SECTION 2. Phrases in Simple Meter with Duple Division of the Beat

For numbers 1–8, follow the procedures outlined in unit 1A, section 2. For the two-part exercises (9–10), follow the procedures outlined in unit 2A, section 2.

1.

2.

3.

4.

5.

6.

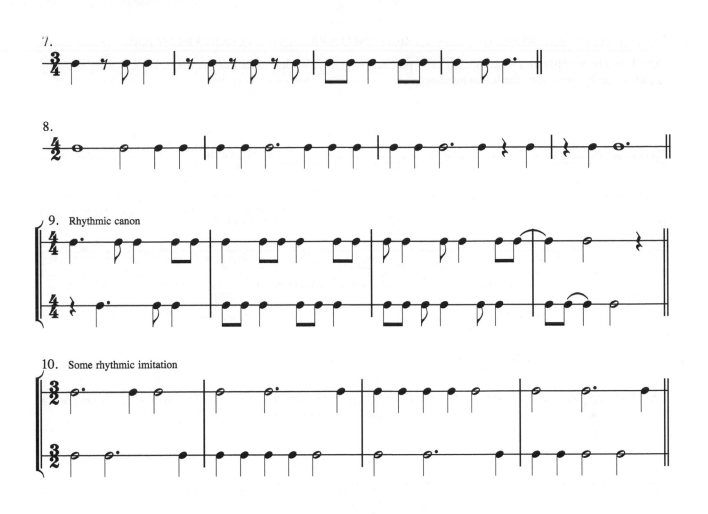

SECTION 3. Creating a Coherent Phrase in Simple Meter

Choose one of the simple meters found in section 1. Using rhythmic patterns provided in section 1, create a coherent four-measure phrase.

Write your solution on the following line (or lines, in case you decided to write a two-voice composition):

B Diatonic Models and Melodic Fragments: P8, P5, P4, M3, m3, M2, and m2

SECTION 1. Diatonic Models

These models anticipate the melodic fragments in the next section.

(A) INTERVALS OUTLINING THE TONIC TRIAD AND DOMINANT 7th CHORD IN MAJOR

Use a D-major vocalise as a warm-up. For extra practice, sing these models in each of the major keys, moving down by fourths or up by fifths. See the following examples:

1.

2.

(B) INTERVALS EMPHASIZING THE TONIC TRIAD IN MINOR, WITH SPECIAL EMPHASIS ON THE PERFECT 4th

Use a D-minor vocalise as a warm-up. For extra practice, sing these models in each of the minor keys, moving down by 5ths or up by 4ths. Follow the same procedure for the D-minor excerpts. See the following examples:

1.

2.

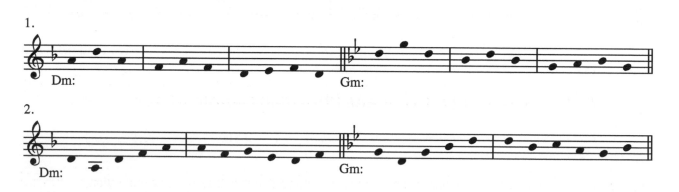

SECTION 2. Melodic Fragments in D Major and D Minor

1. **Andante**

Haydn   Symphony no. 94 (second movement—transposed)

2. **Allegro molto**

Haydn   Symphony no. 94 (third movement—transposed)

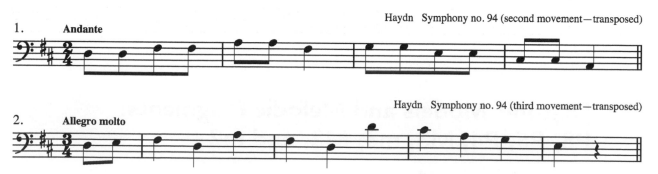

3. **Allegro** — Mozart   Theme (Variations on a Minuet by Duport), K. 573 (adapted and transposed)

Dm:

4. **Allegro** — Mozart   Eight Minuets, K. 315g (adapted and transposed)

Dm:

5. **Adagio** — Bach   Chorale *Nur mein Jesus ist mein Leben* (Only Jesus Is My Life), BWV 490, meas. 1–4 (transposed)

Dm:

6. **Menuetto** — Mozart   Eight Minuets, K. 315g. I, meas. 1–4 (transposed)

7. **Poco Andante** — Beethoven   Piano Sonata op. 81a, II, meas. 176–177 (transposed)

8. **Adagio** — Mozart   Piano Sonata, K. 282 (189g), I, meas. 9–11 (rhythm reduced by half; transposed)

9. **Allegro** — Mozart   Twelve Variations, K. 179 (189a), Variation VIII, meas. 1–4 (transposed) (top line)

10. **Allegro** — Mozart   Twelve Variations, K. 179 (189a), Variation VIII, meas. 1–4 (transposed) (bottom line)

Both lines (9 and 10) should be combined in ensemble.

SECTION 3. Creating a Coherent Melody

Return to section 2 and select two or three segments of melodic fragments that create a coherent melody. It may be necessary to change the meter and rhythm of certain segments, depending on your choice. Here is an example based on measures 1 and 2 of fragment 3 and measures 3 and 4 of fragment 4.

SECTION 4. Improvisation

1. Take melodic fragment 10* as the basis for improvising an upper voice

* Mozart.   Twelve Variations, K 179 (189a), Variation VIII, meas. 1–4 (transposed) (bottom line)

2. Use the upper voice that you have created and improvise a new bass line. (For inspiration you might want to study each of Mozart's 12 Variations K 179 (189a).)

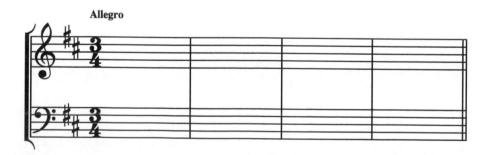

C Melodies (Major): P5, P4, M3, m3, M2, and m2 within the Diatonic Scale

SECTION 1. Melodies by Bruce Benward

Procedure for Completing Each Melody

1. Sing the scale on which the melody is constructed. Use syllables or numbers as suggested by your instructor.
2. When you are familiar with the scale, sing each melody using the same syllables or numbers.
3. Circle the 1st, 3rd, and 5th scale degrees as *reference tones* if you encounter difficulty.
4. Remember that you learn *only* when you sing the correct pitch and syllable or number. So, do not hesitate to repeat a melody until you are satisfied that you have sung it correctly.
5. Tempo is important. Sing each melody slowly at first. If you can increase the tempo without making mistakes, do so.

SECTION 2. Melodies from Folk Sources and Stravinsky

1.

Moderato

"King and Queen"   Florida folk-singing game

From *Games and Songs of American Children,* composed and compiled by William Wells Newell. Copyright, 1883, 1903, by Harper and Brothers, Copyright, 1911, by Robert B. Stone CURWEN & Sons London, Copyright 1914 by Grace Cleveland Porter

2.

Allegro vivace

"La Bastringue"   Old French-Canadian folk-singing game

From *Games and Songs of American Children,* composed and compiled by William Wells Newell. Copyright, 1883, 1903, by Harper and Brothers, Copyright, 1911, by Robert B. Stone CURWEN & Sons London, Copyright 1914 by Grace Cleveland Porter

"Banana Boat Song" Traditional Jamaican

3.

Stravinsky Octet for Wind Instruments (adapted)

4. Tempo guisto ♩ = 116

"The Land of the Humming Bird" (abridged)

5. Moderato

D Melodies (Minor): Mostly by Bruce Benward

SECTION 1. P5, P4, M3, and m3 within the Tonic Triad

1. Sing the scale related to each exercise—as usual, with syllables or numbers.
2. Sing each melody with the same syllables or numbers.
3. For the moment, do not worry about the intervals formed by scale steps 1, 3, and 5. Think of these primarily as *reference tones*—tones from which other scale degrees may be located.

SECTION 2. Natural, Harmonic, and Melodic Minor

The first example shows a single melody repeated to illustrate the three forms of the minor scale. Sing all three forms, one after the other, and note the effect created by each. Examples 2–4 are in natural minor.

1c. Melodic minor

2.

3.

4.

SECTION 3. P5, P4, M3, and m3 within the Tonic Triad and M2 and m2

Follow procedures printed in part D, section 1, of this unit.

1. ♩ = 96

2. ♩ = 96

3. ♩ = 96

4. ♪ = 100

5. ♩ = 63

SECTION 4. Transposition and Inversion

For some additional practice in clef reading and transposition:

1. Transpose number 1 (*Kyrie XI—Orbis factor*). When you visualize the alto clef, think of the melody as being in E minor (Aeolian mode), so include F♯ in the signature.

2. Transpose number 2 (*Sanctus IX—Cum jubilo*). This was originally considered to be in the Ionian mode (now our major mode). When you visualize the alto clef, also add an F♯ to the key signature. The starting note is d'.

3. Melodies 3 and 4 are closely related. The *Kyrie IX* (Cum jubilo) (number 3) is the source for Josquin's *Missa de Beata Virgine* (number 4). The alto voice is shown here. When you visualize the alto clef, see whether you can figure out the correct signatures.

4. Melodies 5 and 6 are from Contrapunctus XII of Bach's *Art of Fugue;* number 6 is the melodic inversion of number 5.

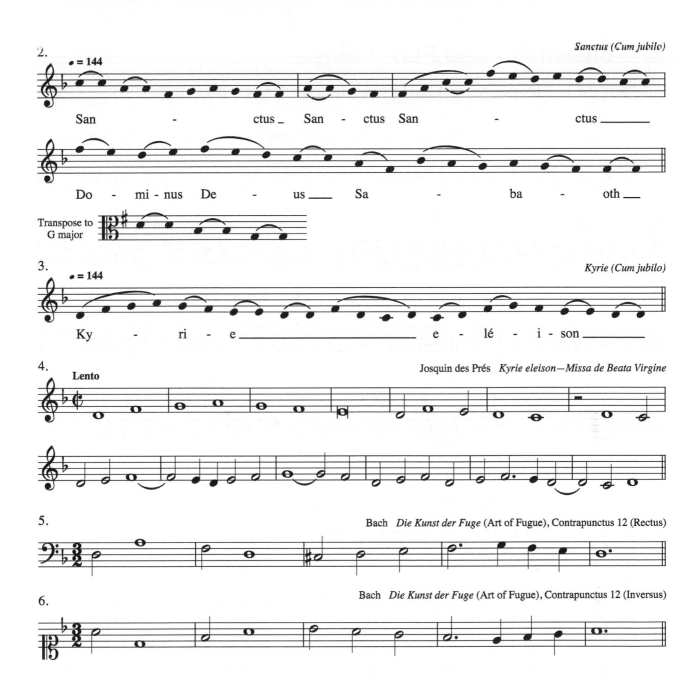

2.   *Sanctus (Cum jubilo)*

San - ctus _ San - ctus San - ctus ___

Do - mi - nus De - us ___ Sa - ba - oth ___

Transpose to
G major

3.   *Kyrie (Cum jubilo)*

Ky - ri - e _____ e - lé - i - son ___

4.   Josquin des Prés   *Kyrie eleison—Missa de Beata Virgine*

Lento

5.   Bach   *Die Kunst der Fuge* (Art of Fugue), Contrapunctus 12 (Rectus)

6.   Bach   *Die Kunst der Fuge* (Art of Fugue), Contrapunctus 12 (Inversus)

E Ensembles and Play + Sing

SECTION 1. Repertoire Using Treble and Bass Clefs

"Come, Thou Fount of Every Blessing" Traditional American melody (Nettleton) (Text: Robinson)

From John Wyeth's Repository of Sacred Music, Part Second 1813, arr. by Phillip Torbert

SECTION 2. Repertoire Using C Clefs

Orlando di Lasso *Cantiones duarum vocum* (Songs for Two Voices), from *Fantasia III*, meas. 1–11

Cantiones duarum vocum from *Fantasia III*, Dessoff Choir Series, edited by Paul Boepple © 1941. Used by permission of Carl Fischer for Mercury Music Corp.

SECTION 3. Play + Sing

Phillip Torbert "Dona nobis pacem"

UNIT FOUR

A Rhythm—Simple Meter: Quadruple Subdivision of the Beat

SECTION 1. Modules in Simple Meter

Using rhythm syllables or a neutral syllable, sing each of the given modules. Begin by repeating each module several times. Then treat the successive modules as a continuous exercise.

In these modules, you are subdividing the beat into four parts, representing the next logical ordering of the beat in the hierarchy of simple meter.

See unit 4C, exercise 1, "Ratta Madan Law"

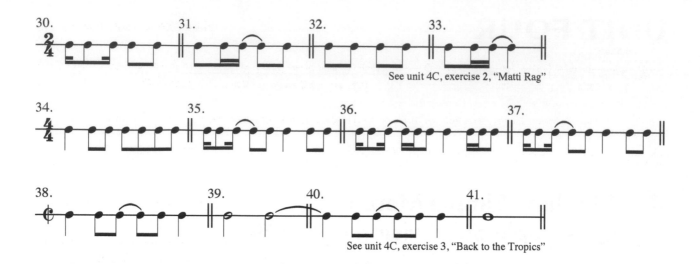

See unit 4C, exercise 2, "Matti Rag"

See unit 4C, exercise 3, "Back to the Tropics"

SECTION 2. Phrases in Simple Meter

For numbers 1–5, follow the procedures outlined in unit 1A, section 2. For the two-part exercises (8–11), follow the procedures outlined in unit 2A, section 2.

6.

Andantino

This is the rhythmic framework for an excerpt from the source by Parisotti that Stravinsky used for Scene 5 of the ballet *Pulcinella*. See the melodic setting in unit 4C1, exercise 4.

For more information, see Maureen Carr's facsimile edition of the *Sources and Sketches for Stravinsky's Pulcinella*, Middleton, Wisconsin: A-R Editions, 2010.

"Skeleton Dance" (adapted)   Creek Ceremonial Song

7. ♩ = 108

This is the rhythmic framework for an excerpt from a ceremonial dance of the Creek Indians. See unit 4C1, exercise 5, "Skeleton Dance."

For more information see Frank G. Speck, *Ceremonial Songs of the Creek and Yuchi Indians*, with music transcribed by Jacob D. Sapir. Philadelphia: Published by the University Museum, 1911, p. 177.

8. Rhythmic canon

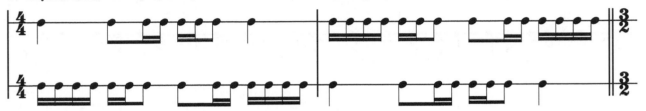

9. Rhythmic canon

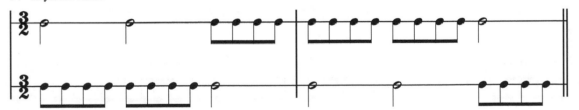

10. Rhythmic framework for Jamaican Folksong

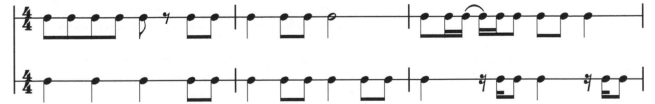

See unit 4E1, exercise 9

11.   Giovanni Pergolesi   *Il Flaminio*, Act 1, Scene 1, Aria (Polidoro)

This is the rhythmic framework for the source by Pergolesi that Stravinsky used for "Serenata" in the ballet *Pulcinella*. See the two-voice melodic setting in unit 4E1, exercise 10.

For more information, see Maureen Carr's facsimile edition of the *Sources and Sketches for Stravinsky's Pulcinella*, Middleton, Wisconsin: A-R Editions, 2010.

SECTION 3. Creating a Coherent Phrase in Simple Meter

Choose one of the simple meters found in section 1. Using rhythmic patterns provided in section 1, create a coherent four-measure phrase.

B Diatonic Models and Melodic Fragments: m10, P8, P5, P4, M3, m3, M2, and m2

SECTION 1. Diatonic Models

These models anticipate the melodic fragments in the next section.

(A) INTERVALS OUTLINING THE TONIC TRIAD AND DOMINANT 7th CHORD

Use an A-major vocalise as a warm-up. For extra practice, sing this model in each of the major keys, using the last note of the pattern as the first note of the same pattern transposed a 4th lower or a 5th higher. See the following model:

AM: EM: BM:

(B) INTERVALS EMPHASIZING THE INTERVALS P4 AND P5, FILLING IN AN OCTAVE

For extra practice, this model can be repeated in all the minor keys by singing the pattern down a P5 (or up a P4) through all 12 keys. See the following model:

Am: Dm: Gm: Cm:

(C) INTERVALS OF THE P5, P4, M3, AND m3, FILLING IN AN OCTAVE

For extra practice, this model may be repeated in all minor keys by singing the pattern down a P5 (up a P4).

Am:

(D) INTERVALS OF THE m10, P4, M3, AND m3 OUTLINING THE TONIC TRIAD

This model provides an unusual example of a tonic triad because the interval of a m10 occurs between the root and the 3rd. For extra practice, repeat this pattern in all minor keys.

Am:

SECTION 2. Melodic Fragments in A Major and A Minor

1. **Allegro** Mozart *Eine kleine Nachtmusik* (A Little Night Music), K. 525 (transposed)

2. **Allegro con brio** Wagner *Die fliegende Holländer*, Overture (first theme transposed)

3. **Allegro** Schubert Symphony no. 5, Minuet (transposed)

4. **Allegro assai** Mozart *Idomeneo*, act I, Aria (Electra) (transposed)

fp

5. **Andante molto moderato** ♩ = 84 Gabriel Fauré *Pavane*, op. 50, meas. 1–5 (transposed) (top line)

6. **Andante molto moderato** ♩ = 84 Gabriel Fauré *Pavane*, op. 50, meas. 1–5 (transposed) (middle line)

7. **Andante molto moderato** ♩ = 84 Gabriel Fauré *Pavane*, op. 50, meas. 1–5 (transposed) (bottom line)

All three lines (5, 6, 7) should be combined in ensemble.

8. **Andantino**   Mozart *Die Zauberflöte* (The Magic Flute), Duet "Pamina, Papageno," meas. 7–9 (transposed) (top line)

9. **Andantino**   Mozart *Die Zauberflöte* (The Magic Flute), Duet "Pamina, Papageno," meas. 23–25 (transposed) (top line)

10.   Mozart *Die Zauberflöte* (The Magic Flute), Duet "Pamina, Papageno," meas. 7–9 (transposed) (bottom line)
Andantino

Two lines can be combined in ensemble (8 and 10; 9 and 10)

SECTION 3. Creating a Coherent Melody

Return to section 2 and select two or three segments of melodic fragments that create a coherent melody. It may be necessary to change the meter and rhythm of certain segments, depending on your choice. Here is an example based on measures 1 and 2 of fragment 2, measures 2 and 3 of fragment 3, and measure 4 of fragment 2.

SECTION 4. Improvisation

1. Take melodic fragment 7 as the basis for improvising an upper voice
   Gabriel Fauré *Pavane*, op. 50, meas. 1–5 (transposed) (bottom line)

2. Use the upper voice that you have created and improvise a new bass line. (For inspiration you might want to study the musical score for Gabriel Fauré's *Pavane,* op. 50.)

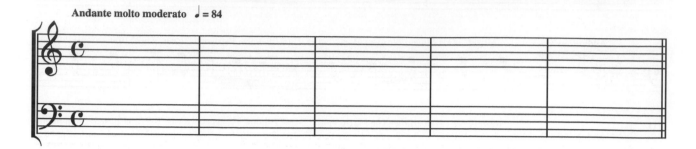

3. Take melodic fragment 10 as the basis for improvising an upper voice
   Mozart *Die Zauberflöte* (The Magic Flute), Duet Pamina, Papageno, meas. 7–9 (transposed) (bottom line)

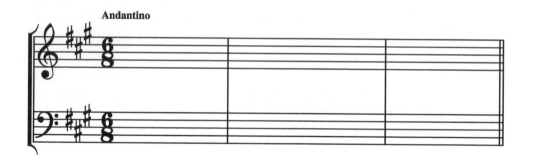

4. Use the upper voice that you have created and improvise a new bass line. (For inspiration you might want to study the musical score for The Magic Flute.)

C   Melodies (Major and Minor): P5, P4, M3, m3, M2, and m2

These melodies are limited to the same skips as those in unit 3C except that the skips may occur between scale degrees other than 1-3-5.

SECTION 1. Jamaican Songs, a Ceremonial Dance and a Stravinsky Source

1.   "Ratta Madan Law"

Jestingly

(Ha   Ha)

(Ha   Ha)   (Ha   Ha)

See unit 4A, exercises 26–29

2.   "Mattie Rag"   (abridged)

See unit 4A, exercises 30–33, and unit 5B, section 2, exercise 8.

"Ratta Madan Law" and "Mattie Rag" from *Jamaica, Land We Love*, compiled by Lloyd Hall.

3.   "Back to the Tropics"

Rhumba tempo

See unit 4, part A, exercises 38–41

4.   Parisotti   "Se tu m'ami" [If you love me]

Andantino   *rit.*

p   *cresc.*

The rhythmic framework for this phrase appeared in Part A2, exercise 6.

5. ♩ = 108   "Skeleton Dance"   Creek Ceremonial Song

The rhythmic framework for this phrase appeared in Part A2, exercise 7.

SECTION 2. Hebrew Songs

1.   "Hevenu Shalom Aleychem" (We Have Brought You Peace)

With spirit

2.   "Adon Olam" (Master of the Universe)

Moderato

3.   "Hin'ni Muchan Um'zuman" (Behold, I Am Prepared and Ready)

Slowly

Fine

1.   2.

1.   2.   D.C. al Fine

7. "Ets Chayim Hi" (It Is a Tree of Life)

8. "Sim Shalom" (Establish Peace)

Exercises 1–8 © 1943 by Jewish Welfare Board, Member Agency USO. Reprinted with permission of the JCC Association.

D Melodies (Major and Minor): P5, P4, M3, m3, M2, and m2

These melodies are limited to the same skips as those of unit 3C, except that the skips may occur between scale degrees other than 1-3-5.

SECTION 1. Songs by Schubert

All melodies in this section are excerpted from the songs of Franz Schubert. Nearly all the rhythm patterns in these songs were already presented, except for the simple triplet in numbers 6 and 9; the three notes of the triplet should be spaced evenly over one complete beat.

Schubert *Der Lindenbaum* (The Linden Tree) from *Winterreise*, op. 89, no. 5, D. 911

6. Mässig

7. Etwas geschwind ♩. = 76

Schubert *Drang in die Ferne* (Urge to Roam), D. 770

Schubert *Der Musensohn* (The Son of the Muses), D. 764a

8. Ziemlich lebhaft

Schubert *Zwei Szenen aus "Lacrimas"* II (Delphine), op. 124, no. 1, D. 857 (2)

9. Mässige Bewegung

SECTION 2. Exercises in Clef Reading and Transposition

This section contains excerpts from the first movement of Schubert's "Unfinished" Symphony.

Procedures

1. Example 1 consists of the opening melody (mm. 13–20), played in unison by two oboes and two clarinets in A. To sing the clarinet part as it sounds, try to think in the soprano clef, with c' (middle C) on the bottom line. Experiment by using letter names and by checking your accuracy with the oboe part. Remember that the oboe is a nontransposing instrument and sounds the same pitches as the clarinet in A.

2. Example 2, from the same movement (mm. 291–298), also features different instruments playing melodies at the same pitch: violas (Vla) and cellos (Vc). Because these instruments are nontransposing, it is not necessary for you to use clefs for the purpose of changing key. Cello parts are sometimes written in the tenor clef but most often in the bass clef.

3. In this excerpt, the same melodic figure appears four times. For the purposes of this exercise, it is advised to consider the following temporary tonic pitches:

    mm. 291–292—F♯ minor
    mm. 293–294—E major
    mm. 295–296—C♯ minor
    mm. 297–298—B major

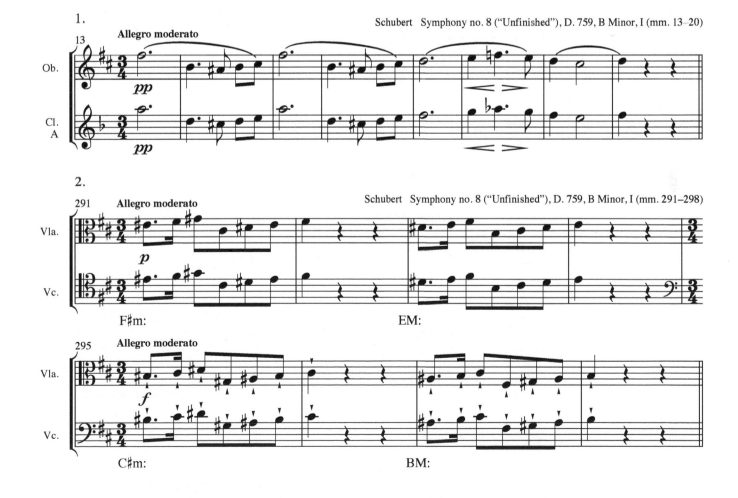

UNIT 4   67

E Ensembles and Play + Sing

SECTION 1. Repertoire Using Treble and Bass Clefs

The first eight excerpts are from chorale melodies harmonized by Bach. The ninth excerpt represents the outer voices of a Jamaican folk song. The rhythmic framework for this excerpt was presented in part A, section 2, number 8 of this unit. A tempo of ♩ = 72–80 is suggested for all of these examples. The tenth excerpt represents the source by Pergolesi that Stravinsky used for "Serenata" in the ballet *Pulcinella*. The rhythmic framework was provided in Part A2, exercise 11.

For more information, see Maureen Carr's facsimile edition of the *Sources and Sketches for Stravinsky's Pulcinella*, Middleton, Wisconsin: A-R Editions, 2010.

Follow the procedures outlined in unit 1E, for ensemble singing.

9. **With disdain**   Jamaica

bass line adapted

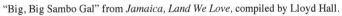

See unit 4A2, exercise 10

"Big, Big Sambo Gal" from *Jamaica, Land We Love,* compiled by Lloyd Hall.

Pergolesi   *Il Flaminio*, Act 1, Scene 1, Aria (Polidoro)

10. **Larghetto** ♩. = 50

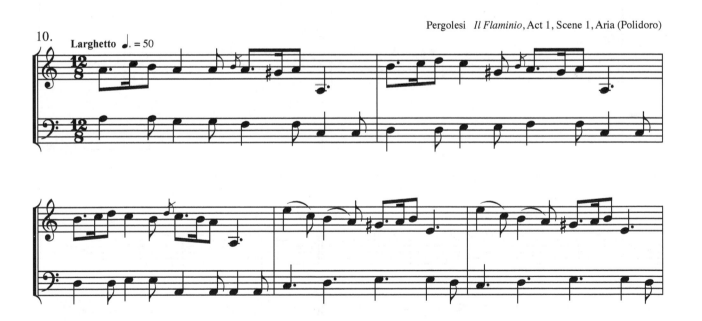

See unit 4A2, exercise 11

SECTION 2. Repertoire Using C Clefs

For the following example from Haydn's String Quartet op. 17, no. 5, Minuet and Trio, students are invited to bring their instruments to class.

Haydn   String Quartet op. 17, no. 5, II

Attacca subito il Menuetto

SECTION 3. Play + Sing

Haydn "Drumroll" Symphony (op. 103/ii, meas. 1–4, adapted)

1.

Andante più tosto Allegretto

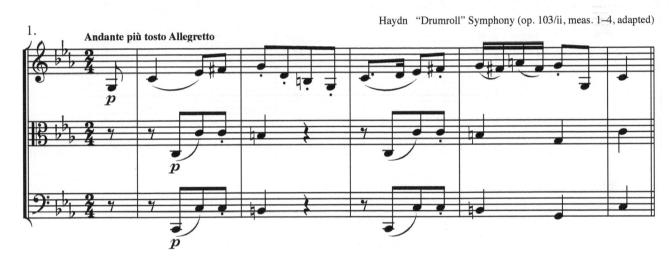

2.

Menuetto

UNIT FIVE

A Rhythm—Simple Meter with Triplets

SECTION 1. Modules in Simple Meter

Using rhythm syllables or a neutral syllable, sing each of the given modules. Begin by repeating each module several times. Then treat the successive modules as a continuous exercise.

In these modules, we are introducing the triplet, which represents an irregular division of the beat in simple meter.

SECTION 2. Phrases in Simple Meter with Irregular Division of the Beat (the Triplet)

For numbers 1–4, follow the procedures outlined in unit 1A, section 2. For the two-part exercises (5–6), follow the procedures outlined in unit 2A, section 2.

5. Rhythmic ostinato

6. Rhythmic canon

SECTION 3. Creating a Coherent Phrase in Simple Meter with Triplets

Using the rhythmic patterns provided in section 1, create a coherent four-measure phrase.

Write your solution on the following line:

B Diatonic Models and Melodic Fragments: M6 and m6

SECTION 1. Diatonic Models

These models anticipate the melodic fragments in the next section.

These exercises emphasize intervals of the major 6th (M6) from scale degree 5 (C) in an ascending motion to scale degree 3 (A) before moving in a descending motion to scale degree 1 (F). Follow the same procedure as in previous units. For extra practice, sing these exercises in all major keys, transposing to each new key by P5s down or P4s up.

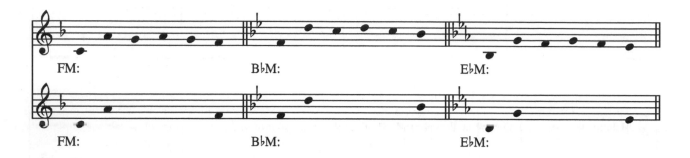

This model opens with the ascending M6 from scale degree 5 (C) up to scale degree 3 (A) and continues in an ascending motion to scale degree 1 (F).

Here the minor 6th (m6) is a chordal skip. The m6 (F down to A) functions as a consonant skip in support of the final pitch, C.

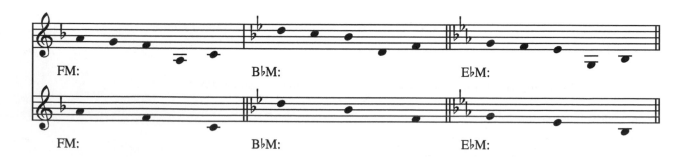

In this set, the major 6th (M6) is part of III in pure (natural) minor.

Dm: III   i   Gm: III   i   Cm: III   i   Fm: III   i

The sequential relationship of these exercises (F major) with triads on F and D is similar to that of the previous example, except that the tonic of the previous exercise is D minor. Use the same procedures as earlier.

FM: BbM: EbM:

These exercises outline the D-minor tonic triad. In this section, which serves as preparation for the singing of the melodic fragments, the authors recommend drills in relative minor rather than parallel minor because of the tonal design of melodic fragments 4 and 5, which begin in F major and end in D minor.

Dm: Gm: Cm:

This exercise introduces the M6 as a descending pattern from scale degree 3 (A) to scale degree 5 (C), first as part of a triadic pattern and then in combination with a m6 from scale degree 6 (D) to scale degree 4 (Bb).

FM: BbM: EbM:

SECTION 2. Melodic Fragments in F Major and D Minor

Chopin Nocturne op. 9, no. 2 (transposed)

1. **Andante** ♪ = 132

Chopin Nocturne op. 62, no. 2 (transposed)

2. **Lento**

Chopin Nocturne op. 27, no. 2 (transposed)

3.
Lento sostenuto ♩. = 50

4.
Lento ♩. = 60

Chopin Nocturne op. 15, no. 3 (transposed)

5.
Chopin Nocturne op. 55, no. 2 (transposed)

Lento sostenuto

6.
Allegro molto agitato ♩. = 96

Chopin Etude op. 10, no. 9 (transposed)

7.
In a carefree style

Jamaica "Mattie walla lef"

From *Jamaica, Land We Love,* compiled by Lloyd Hall.

8.
Not too fast

Jamaica "Mattie Rag" (transposed)

See unit 4C, exercise 2.

From *Jamaica, Land We Love,* compiled by Lloyd Hall.

9.
Slowish ♩ = 54

Grainger *Colonial Song*

10.
Flowingly ♩ = 80–88

Grainger *Irish Tune from County Derry*

Irish Tune from County Derry. Copyright 1930 by Percy Grainger, International Copyright secured. Printed in the USA. G. Schirmer, Inc.

SECTION 3. Creating a Coherent Melody

Return to section 2 and select two or three segments of melodic fragments that create a coherent melody. It may be necessary to change the meter and rhythm of certain segments, depending on your choice.

SECTION 4. Improvisation

1. The following accompaniment figure is adapted from Chopin's Nocturne opus 27, no. 2 (transposed). Recall that melodic fragment 3 is from the same piece. Use the accompaniment figure as the basis for improvising an upper voice.

2. Use the upper voice that you have created and improvise a new bass line. (For inspiration, you might want to study the musical score for several of Chopin's Nocturnes.)

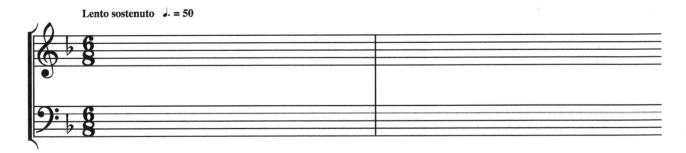

3. The following accompaniment figure is adapted from Chopin's Nocturne opus 9, no. 2 (transposed). Recall that melodic fragment 1 is from the same piece. Use the accompaniment figure as the basis for improvising an upper voice.

4. Use the upper voice that you have created and improvise a new bass line. (For inspiration, you might want to study the musical score for several of Chopin's Nocturnes.)

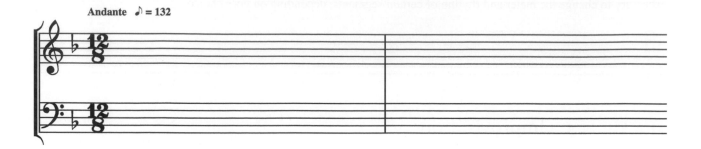

C Melodies (Major and Minor): M6 and m6

The next five songs are from a collection titled *Six Creole Folk-Songs* (music arranged and translations by Maud Cuney Hare). Some of the rhythmic and melodic fragments found in these songs emphasize the models of parts A and B of this unit.

"Quand mo-té jeune" (Bal fini) (Dance song)

3. Con moto ♩ = 116

"Aine, dé, trois, Caroline" (Song of Longing)

4. Allegro ♩ = 92

5.

Exercises 1–5 from *Six Creole Folk-Songs*. Music arranged and translations by Maud Cuney Hare © by Carl Fischer, New York, 1921.

D Melodies (Major and Minor): M6 and m6

The format of this section resembles that of part B ("Diatonic Models and Melodic Fragments for Interval Singing") in that selected melodies are written in or transposed to the same key. Here, the melodies are in either G major or E minor. Because of the nature of these songs, it is an advantage to study them within the framework of the same key signature. For example, the key signature of E minor helps clarify the similarity between melodic patterns in two selections that are in natural minor: number 1, "Monday, Tuesday," from Ireland, and number 2, "The Laughter of Raindrops," from Jamaica. The modal flavor of the subtonic triad (D, F♯, A) in relation to the tonic triad (E, G, B) provides the link of continuity between these songs. In this section, some of the major melodies tilt toward relative minor and some of the minor melodies toward relative major.

Traditional "Da Luain, da Mairt" (Monday, Tuesday) Southern Counties, Ireland (transposed)

1.

2.

"The Laughter of Raindrops" Music by Kathleen McFarlane, Words by Lisa Salmon. From *Jamaica, Land We Love*, compiled by Lloyd Hall.

Andrea Gabrieli (uncle of Giovanni Gabrieli) "A caso un giorno" (One Day by Chance), from *First Book of Madrigals* for three voices
(transposed)*

3.

Adapted from "A caso un giorno," by Andrea Gabrieli and published in *Andrea Gabrieli: Complete Madrigals 1:* Madrigals of Libro primo a 3;
Canzone of Petrarch a 3; Giustiniane a 3; edited by Tillman Merritt. Recent Researches in the Music of the Renaissance, vol. 41. Madison,
Wisconsin: A-R Editions, Inc. 1981. Used with permission.

*Melody only.

4.

Bold with well defined rhythm

Kathleen McFarlane (Jamaica)   "Henry Morgan" (abridged) (transposed)

"Henry Morgan" music by Kathleen McFarlane, from *Jamaica, Land We Love,* compiled by Lloyd Hall.

5.

Ireland   "A New Song Called Granuaile"

6.

Andante

"I Will Walk with My Love" (a fragment)   County Dublin, Ireland   (transposed)

7.   Ireland "The Piper's Tunes"

Chorus

Ri - too-ral-oo-ral - ah,   Ri -

too-ral-oo-ral - ad - dy, Ri - too-ral-oo-ral - ah Ri - too-ral-oo-ral - ad - dy.

8.   Ireland "Lillibulero" (transposed)

Chorus

Lè - ro lè - ro   lè - ro lè - ro   Lil - li - bu - lè - ro bul - len a la

Lil - li bu - lè - ro   lè - ro lè - ro   Lil - li bu - lè ro bul - len a la

9.

Jamaican Folk Song   "Cudelia Brown" (transposed)

From *Jamaica, Land We Love*, compiled by Lloyd Hall.

E Ensembles and Play + Sing

SECTION 1. Repertoire Using Treble and Bass Clefs

Andrea Gabrieli   "Che giova posseder" (What Good Does It Do to Possess Cities and Kingdoms)

gni,   E pa - la - gi ha-bi - tar   d'al - to la - vo -

gni, E   pa - la - gi ha-bi - tar   d'al - to la - vo -

gni,   E pa - la - gi ha-bi - tar   d'al - to   la - vo -

ro,   E ser - vi in - tor - no ha-ver d'im - pe - rio de - gni   Et   l'ar - che

ro,   E ser - vi in - tor - no ha - ver d'im - pe - rio de - gni   Et l'ar - che

ro,   E ser - vi in - tor - no ha-ver d'im - pe - rio de - gni, Et   l'ar - che

gra - vi   per mol - to the - so   - ro,   Es -

gra - vi   per mol - to the - so   - ro, Es - ser can -

gra - vi per mol - to the - so   - ro,

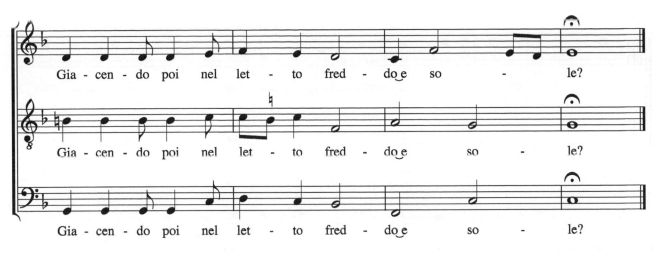

Adapted from "Che giova posseder," by Andrea Gabrieli, and published in *Andrea Gabrieli: Complete Madrigals 1:* Madrigals of Libro primo a 3; Canzone of Petrarch a 3; Giustiniane a 3; edited by Tillman Merritt. Recent Researches in the Music of the Renaissance, vol. 41. Madison, Wisconsin: A-R Editions, Inc. 1981. Used with permission.

SECTION 2. Repertoire Using C Clefs

In the following Ballade no. 11 "N'en fait n'en dit, n'en pensee" (Nothing Done, Nothing Said, Nothing Thought) written by Guillaume de Machaut in the fourteenth century, the lower voice was intended to be performed by an instrument to accompany the upper line. Students should be reminded to bring their instruments to class to provide accompaniment to the vocal line.

Machaut "N'en fait n'en dit n'en pensee" (Nothing Done, Nothing Said, Nothing Thought) from the *Complete Works of Machaut,*
edited by Friedrich Ludwig, vol. I, B11, p. 10

Printed with the friendly permission of Breitkopf & Härtel, Wiesbaden.

Felix Mendelssohn Song without Words, op. 30, no. 6, "Venetianisches Gondellied" (adapted)

1.

Breitkopf & Härtel, 1874–77

2.

UNIT SIX

A Rhythm—Simple Meter: Further Subdivision of the Beat in Simple Meter

SECTION 1. Modules in Simple Meter

Using rhythm syllables or a neutral syllable, sing each of the given modules. Begin by repeating each module several times. Then treat the successive modules as a continuous exercise.

Just as in the modules of unit 4, we are subdividing the beat into four parts.

Compare modules 23–28 to section 2, exercise 9.

SECTION 2. Phrases in Simple Meter

1.

2. Rhythmic crescendo and decrescendo

3.

4.

5.

6. Alternating $\frac{2}{4}$ and $\frac{3}{4}$; see "The Raftsmen's Song," in this unit

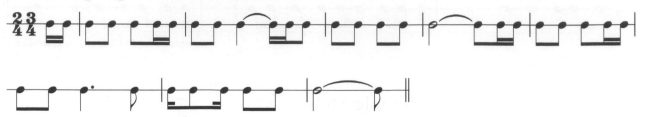

7. The upper voice is a rhythmic augmentation of the first four bars of the lower voice.

8. Rhythmic ostinato

Adapted from *The Music of Santería,* pp. 109–110. *Traditional Rhythms of the Batá Drums,* by John Amira and Steven Cornelius (Crown Point, Ind. White Cliffs Media Company, 1992). "This book presents the salute (or praise) rhythms of batá drumming. The most sacred and complex of the ritual music associated with the Afro-Cuban religion Santería" (p. 1). "Batá are double-headed, hourglass shaped drums" (p. 15). "Ochún—a river deity, Ochún is the goddess of love and beauty" (p. 109).

9. Ochun

$\quad$=100

SECTION 3. Creating a Coherent Phrase in Simple Meter

Using the rhythmic patterns provided in section 1, create a coherent four-measure phrase.

Write your solution on the following line:

B Diatonic Models and Melodic Fragments: M6 and m6

SECTION 1. Diatonic Models

These models anticipate the melodic fragments in the next section. These exercises emphasize intervals of the chordal skips within a major tonic triad starting with the root, moving down to the 5th and then up to the 3rd. The upward skip from scale degree 5 to scale degree 3 results in the interval of a major 6th (M6). Follow the same procedure as in previous units. For extra practice, sing these exercises in all major keys, transposing to each new key by P5s down or P4s up. The tossing of triads among students should continue, as shown in the following model:

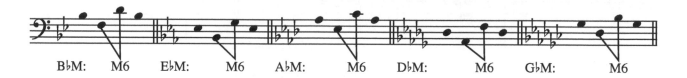

The first three melodic fragments (Mozart, Beethoven, and Makeba) follow a similar melodic contour.

These exercises emphasize the chordal skips within a major tonic triad, starting with the root, moving to the 3rd, and then down to the 5th. The downward skip from scale degree 3 to scale degree 5 results in a major 6th (M6). Follow the same procedures as in previous units. Sing the model in all major keys, transposing in the manner described in each previous unit.

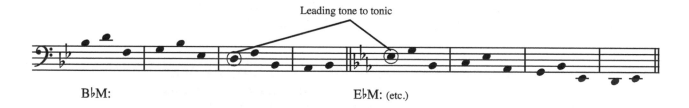

The tonic and subdominant triads are outlined. The dominant is implied only with the leading tone as it progresses to tonic.

These exercises combine the major and minor 6th patterns that form the basis of melodic fragments 5, 6, and 7. Follow the same procedure as described in previous units, using the following model as the basis for transposition.

3.   "The Raftsmen's Song"

"The Raftsmen's Song" from *Lumbering Songs from the Northern Woods* by Edith Fowke, Tunes transcribed by Norman Cazden.
Published for the American Folklore Society by the University of Texas Press, Austin and London: copyright 1970 by the American Folklore
Society Memoir Series, Wm. Hugh Jansen, General Editor, vol. 55, 1970.

4.   "Z'Basel an mym Rhy"

Songs 5–8 in this section include songs by the trouvéres of the twelfth and thirteenth century France—in chronological order: Richard the Lion-hearted (1157–1199); Gace Brulé (1160–1213); Thibaut IV, King of Navarre (1201–1253). These melodies, including the one that is anonymous, are taken from the 1927 edition published by the University of Pennsylvania Press (printed in U. S. A. 1964), vol. II titled *L'Édition du Corpus Cantilenarum Medii Aevi*. The numbers that appear together with each song are those of the 1927 (1964 printing) edition.

5.   Thibaut IV, King of Navarre   "Pastorelle" (Pastoral), No. 142

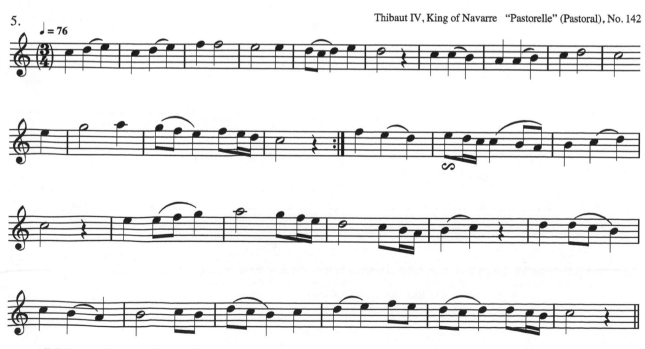

"Pastorelle" No. 142 from *Les Chansonniers des Troubadours et des Trouvéres*, vol. 2, 1927. Reprinted by permission of the University of Pennsylvania Press.

This model emphasizes the ascending major 6th (M6), followed by a descending scale line, and may be thought of in Bb major as well as G minor. This exercise is related to fragments 8–10.

SECTION 2.   Melodic Fragments in B♭ Major and B♭ Minor

1.   Mozart   *Requiem*, K. 626, *Tuba Mirum*
   Andante

2.   Beethoven   *Fidelio* (Overture), op. 72C (transposed and adapted)
   Allegro

3.   African Folk Song   Makeba   "Dubula" (Shoot) (transposed)

4.   Mozart   Minuet, K. 2, no. 2 (transposed)
   Allegro

5.   Mussorgsky   *Boris Godounov* (Opera), Scene 2 (transposed)
   Moderato

6.   Mozart   *Requiem*, K. 626, *Lacrymosa* (Tears) (transposed)
   Larghetto

7.   Schubert   Variation on a Waltz by Diabelli, D. 718 (transposed)
   Andante

8.   Tchaikovsky   Symphony no. 5, op. 64 (transposed)
   Andante

9. **Allegro**   Mozart Six German Dances, no. v, K. 509 (transposed)

10. **With easy gaiety**   Mahler *Wer hat dies Liedlein erdacht* (Up There on the Hill) from *Des Knaben Wunderhorn* (The Youth's Magic Horn) (transposed)

SECTION 3. Creating a Coherent Melody

Return to section 2 and select two or three segments of melodic fragments that create a coherent melody. It may be necessary to change the meter and rhythm of certain segments, depending on your choice.

SECTION 4. Improvisation

The following bass line is taken from the Tenor *David* used by Machaut as the basis for a "double hocket." Twenty-two measures are provided in this excerpt. Notice that the rhythmic *talea* extends from measures 1–11 and that the same succession of rhythmic values recurs in measures 12–22. All three voices of measures 1–22 appear in part E, section 2 of this unit. Before looking at Machaut's complete realization of this excerpt, use this "isorhythmic bass" line as a basis for creating one upper voice. Then create a new isorhythmic bass to accompany the newly created upper voice.

Machaut Tenor *David*

Printed with the friendly permission of Breitkopf & Härtel, Wiesbaden.

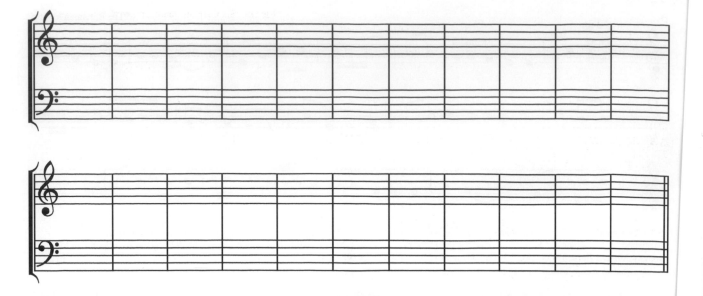

C Melodies (Major and Minor): M6 and m6

Songs 1–4 in this section include folk songs from the northern woods of the United States and the cities of Basel and Lausanne, Switzerland. Some of the rhythm and melodic fragments found in these songs emphasize the models of parts A and B of this unit.

1. ♩ = 138   "I Am a River Driver"

"I Am a River Driver" from *Lumbering Songs from the Northern Woods* by Edith Fowke, Tunes transcribed by Norman Cazden. Published for the American Folklore Society by the University of Texas Press, Austin and London: copyright 1970 by the American Folklore Society Memoir Series, Wm. Hugh Jansen, General Editor, vol. 55, 1970.

2. ♩ = 60   "How We Got Up to the Woods Last Year"

"How We Got Up to the Woods Last Year" from *Lumbering Songs from the Northern Woods* by Edith Fowke, Tunes transcribed by Norman Cazden. Published for the American Folklore Society by the University of Texas Press, Austin and London: copyright 1970 by the American Folklore Society Memoir Series, Wm. Hugh Jansen, General Editor, vol. 55, 1970.

3.

= 88

"The Raftsmen's Song" from *Lumbering Songs from the Northern Woods* by Edith Fowke, Tunes transcribed by Norman Cazden.
Published for the American Folklore Society by the University of Texas Press, Austin and London: copyright 1970 by the American Folklore
Society Memoir Series, Wm. Hugh Jansen, General Editor, vol. 55, 1970.

4.

"Z'Basel an mym Rhy"

= 76

Songs 5–8 in this section include songs by the trouvéres of the twelfth and thirteenth century France—in chronological order: Richard the Lion-hearted (1157–1199); Gace Brulé (1160–1213); Thibaut IV, King of Navarre (1201–1253).
These melodies, including the one that is anonymous, are taken from the 1927 edition published by the University of
Pennsylvania Press (printed in U. S. A. 1964), vol. II titled *L'Édition du Corpus Cantilenarum Medii Aevi.* The numbers that appear together with each song are those of the 1927 (1964 printing) edition.

5.

Thibaut IV, King of Navarre   "Pastorelle" (Pastoral), No. 142

= 76

"Pastorelle" No. 142 from *Les Chansonniers des Troubadours et des Trouvéres,* vol. 2, 1927. Reprinted by permission of the University of
Pennsylvania Press.

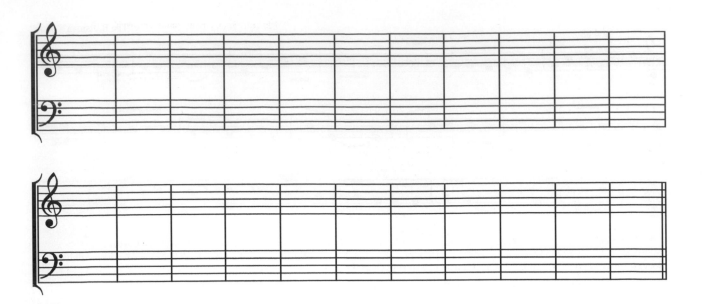

C Melodies (Major and Minor): M6 and m6

Songs 1–4 in this section include folk songs from the northern woods of the United States and the cities of Basel and Lausanne, Switzerland. Some of the rhythm and melodic fragments found in these songs emphasize the models of parts A and B of this unit.

1. "I Am a River Driver"

"I Am a River Driver" from *Lumbering Songs from the Northern Woods* by Edith Fowke, Tunes transcribed by Norman Cazden. Published for the American Folklore Society by the University of Texas Press, Austin and London: copyright 1970 by the American Folklore Society Memoir Series, Wm. Hugh Jansen, General Editor, vol. 55, 1970.

2. "How We Got Up to the Woods Last Year"

"How We Got Up to the Woods Last Year" from *Lumbering Songs from the Northern Woods* by Edith Fowke, Tunes transcribed by Norman Cazden. Published for the American Folklore Society by the University of Texas Press, Austin and London: copyright 1970 by the American Folklore Society Memoir Series, Wm. Hugh Jansen, General Editor, vol. 55, 1970.

9. Allegro

Mozart Six German Dances, no. v, K. 509 (transposed)

Mahler *Wer hat dies Liedlein erdacht* (Up There on the Hill) from *Des Knaben Wunderhorn* (The Youth's Magic Horn) (transposed)

10. With easy gaiety

SECTION 3. Creating a Coherent Melody

Return to section 2 and select two or three segments of melodic fragments that create a coherent melody. It may be necessary to change the meter and rhythm of certain segments, depending on your choice.

SECTION 4. Improvisation

The following bass line is taken from the Tenor *David* used by Machaut as the basis for a "double hocket." Twenty-two measures are provided in this excerpt. Notice that the rhythmic *talea* extends from measures 1–11 and that the same succession of rhythmic values recurs in measures 12–22. All three voices of measures 1–22 appear in part E, section 2 of this unit. Before looking at Machaut's complete realization of this excerpt, use this "isorhythmic bass" line as a basis for creating one upper voice. Then create a new isorhythmic bass to accompany the newly created upper voice.

Machaut Tenor *David*

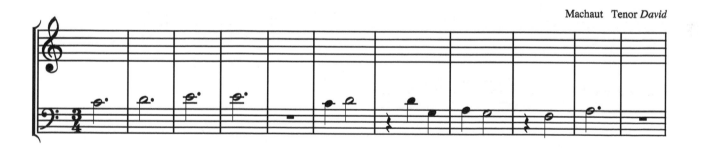

Printed with the friendly permission of Breitkopf & Härtel, Wiesbaden.

This model emphasizes the ascending major 6th (M6), followed by a descending scale line, and may be thought of in Bb major as well as G minor. This exercise is related to fragments 8–10.

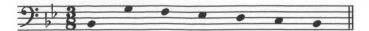

SECTION 2. Melodic Fragments in B♭ Major and B♭ Minor

1. **Andante** — Mozart *Requiem,* K. 626, *Tuba Mirum*

2. **Allegro** — Beethoven *Fidelio* (Overture), op. 72C (transposed and adapted)

3. (♩ = 160) — African Folk Song Makeba "Dubula" (Shoot) (transposed)

4. **Allegro** — Mozart Minuet, K. 2, no. 2 (transposed)

5. **Moderato** — Mussorgsky *Boris Godounov* (Opera), Scene 2 (transposed)

6. **Larghetto** — Mozart *Requiem,* K. 626, *Lacrymosa* (Tears) (transposed)

7. **Andante** — Schubert Variation on a Waltz by Diabelli, D. 718 (transposed)

8. **Andante** (♩ = 80) — Tchaikovsky Symphony no. 5, op. 64 (transposed)

6. ♩ = 76

"Chanson" (Song) No. 152 from *Les Chansonniers des Troubadours et des Trouvéres*, vol. 2, 1927. Reprinted by permission of the University of Pennsylvania Press.

Gace Brulé   (?) "Chanson" (Song), No. 59

7. ♩ = 76

"Chanson" (Song) No. 59 from *Les Chansonniers des Troubadours et des Trouvéres*, vol. 2, 1927. Reprinted by permission of the University of Pennsylvania Press.

Gace Brulé   "Chanson" (Song), No. 60

8. ♩ = 76

"Chanson" (Song) No. 60 from *Les Chansonniers des Troubadours et des Trouvéres*, vol. 2, 1927. Reprinted by permission of the University of Pennsylvania Press.

D Melodies (Major and Minor): M6 and m6

SECTION 1. Robert Schumann

The melodies in this section are taken from instrumental works by Robert Schumann. The first two selections from Schumann's *Album for the Young,* op. 68, provide further exercises in clef reading.

Example 1:   This excerpt is in A B A form. The melody of the B section is almost the same as A except that it centers around G as tonic rather than C. With the return of the original material in the final A, the bass clef is used to illustrate the 5th relationship between the bass and tenor clefs. Sing these two lines an octave higher.

Example 2:   Line 2 is almost identical to line 1, except for its octave transposition, and allows you to check to see whether you are reading the clef correctly. The only new clef is the mezzo-soprano clef, which places middle C (c') on the second line up from the lowest.

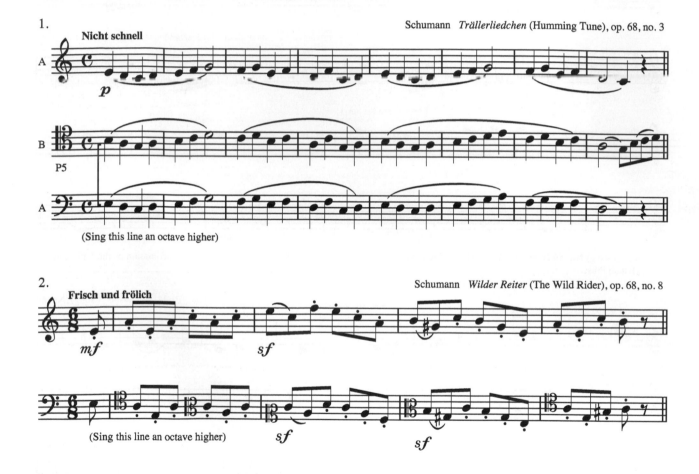

1.

Schumann *Trällerliedchen* (Humming Tune), op. 68, no. 3

(Sing this line an octave higher)

2.

Schumann *Wilder Reiter* (The Wild Rider), op. 68, no. 8

(Sing this line an octave higher)

The clef reading strategies outlined for examples 1 and 2 should be applied to melodies 3–10, also by Schumann.

Schumann *Papillons* (Butterflies), op. 2, no. 3

3.

Schumann *Papillons* (Butterflies), op. 2, no. 12 (Finale)

4.

Schumann *Stückchen* (A Little Piece), op. 68, no. 5

5. **Nicht schnell**

Schumann #5 from *Albumblätter* (Album Leaves), op. 99, no. 8

6. **Langsam**

Schumann *Scherzo* op. 99, no. 13

7. **Lebhaft**

Schumann *Kleine Romanze* (Little Romance), op. 68, no. 19 (transposed) (abridged)

8. **Nicht sehr schnell** ♩ = 130

Schumann *Ernteliedchen* (Harvest Song), op. 68, no. 24 (transposed) (abridged)

9. **Mit fröhlichem Ausdruck**

Schumann *Schnitterliedchen* (The Reapers' Song), op. 68, no. 18

10. **Nicht sehr schnell**

SECTION 2. From Bach to Barber

The six melodies in this section are from works by various composers from Bach to Barber.

Transpose this familiar Rossini tune up a minor 2nd to F major, starting on note C, by reading in the alto clef (displaced by an octave).

Rossini *William Tell* Overture, R-10

1. **Allegro vivace**

ff

* Ten measures omitted

pp

Schubert *Ecossaise* 1, D. 421

2.

*f

(mm. 1–4) * octave lower than original

Bach English Suite III, Gavotte II (or Musette)

3.

*(eight measures omitted)

Bach Brandenburg Concerto no. 2, I (transposed down two octaves)

4.

Johannes Brahms Theme from Symphony No. 1 in C minor, fourth movement, op. 68, meas. 61–78 (transposed from C major)

5.

poco *f*

sf

p

6. In waltz time ♩ = 112
m.7

Barber "Under the Willow Tree" from *Vanessa*

E Ensembles and Play + Sing

SECTION 1. Repertoire Using Treble and Bass Clefs

This section begins with settings of the *Kyrie* and *Christe* from the *Litany of the Blessed Virgin Mary* by Johann de Fossa together with the sources from Gregorian chant. (Other excerpts of chant were given in Unit 1 B, Section 2.) The other excerpt is from a work by Beethoven.

1.

Johann de Fossa *Litania de B.V.M.* (Litany of the Blessed Virgin Mary)

Ky - ri - e e - lei - son.

Ky - ri - e e - lei - son.

Ky - ri - e e - lei - son.

Ky - ri - e e - lei - son.

Ky - ri - e e - lei - son.

Chri - ste _____ e - lei - son.

Chri - ste _____ e - lei - son.

Chri - ste _____ e - lei - son.

Chri - ste _____ e - lei - son.

Chri - ste _____ e - lei - son.

Ky - ri - e e - lei - son.

Ky - ri - e e - lei - son.

Ky - ri - e e - lei - son.

Ky - ri - e e - lei - son.

Ky - ri - e e - lei - son.

1. Chri - ste _____ au - di nos.
2. Chri - ste ex - au - di nos.

1. Chri - ste _____ au - di nos.
2. Chri - ste ex - au - di nos.

1. Chri - ste _____ au - di nos.
2. Chri - ste ex - au - di nos.

1. Chri - ste _____ au - di nos.
2. Chri - ste ex - au - di nos.

1. Chri - ste _____ au - di nos.
2. Chri - ste ex - au - di nos.

Adapted from *Litania de B.V.M.* by Johann de Fossa, and published in *Johann de Fossa: The Collected Works*, edited by Egbert M. Ennulat. Recent Researches in the Music of the Renaissance, vols. 28–29. Madison, Wisconsin: A-R Editions, Inc. 1978. Used with permission.

2. Beethoven   Sonata for Piano and Cello, op. 69, I (transposed from E major)

Allegro ma non tanto

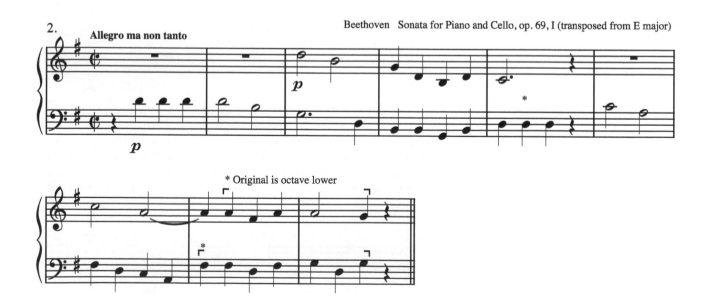

* Original is octave lower

SECTION 2. Repertoire Using C Clefs

The first excerpt is from a Mozart string quartet and can be used as a choral or instrumental exercise, or both.

Mozart String Quartet, K. 458, I (transposed)

The second excerpt is related to the improvisation exercise introduced earlier in this unit (part B, section 4), based on the Tenor *David*. Here, you will find the same isorhythmic bass of 22 measures with two statements of the rhythmic *talea*. It serves as the accompaniment for the two-voice hocket by Machaut. For information about the cultural context for this work, students are invited to read Chapter 8: "Machaut's *David Hocket* and the coronation of Charles V (1364)" in a book titled *Guillaume de Machaut and Reims: Context and Meaning in His Musical Works,* by Ann Walters Robertson and published in 2002 by Cambridge University Press.

In 1981, Harrison Birtwistle wrote a modern arrangement of *Hoquetus David. Instrumental Motet. Guillaume de Machaut.*

Students should be encouraged to bring their instruments to class.

2.   Machaut *Hoquetus David* (David Hocket)

Printed with the friendly permission of Breitkopf & Härtel, Wiesbaden.

SECTION 3. Play + Sing

1.

Bach "Wachet auf" from Cantata No. 140, BWV 140, meas. 1–13

2.

UNIT SEVEN

A Rhythm—Hemiola

SECTION 1. Modules Using Hemiola

Using rhythm syllables or a neutral syllable, sing each of the given modules. Begin by repeating each module several times, then treat the successive modules as a continuous exercise.

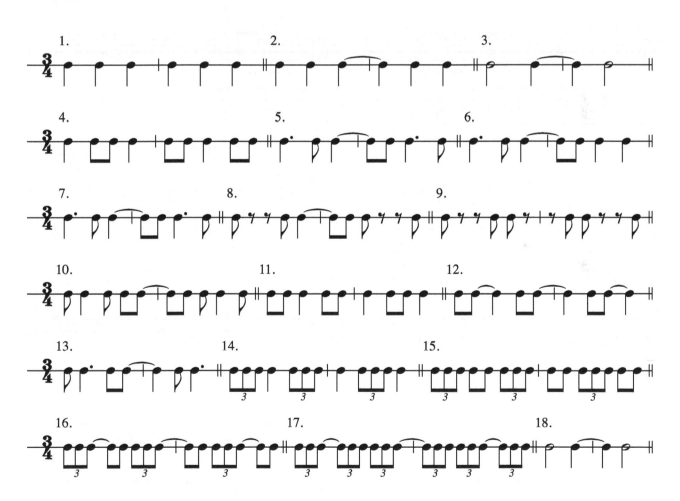

SECTION 2. Phrases in Simple Meter Using Hemiola

Joseph Lanner *Pester Walzer*, op. 93, no. 1

1.

Carl Orff "Odi et amo" from *Catulli Carmina*

2.

SECTION 3. Creating a Coherent Phrase in Simple Meter

Using the rhythmic patterns provided in section 1, create a coherent four-measure phrase.

Write your solution on the following line:

B Diatonic Models and Melodic Fragments: m7

SECTION 1. Diatonic Models

The exercises in this section relate to the music of Haydn, Mozart, and Beethoven, with particular emphasis on the minor 7th. The musical fragments that correspond with these exercises are quoted in section 2.

The two models that follow are related to the Haydn and Mozart fragments (nos. 1 and 2). Treat these models as exercises in antiphonal singing by having half the class sing "a" and the other half answer by singing "b." Continue this process in all major keys, transposing to each new key by P5s down or P4s up.

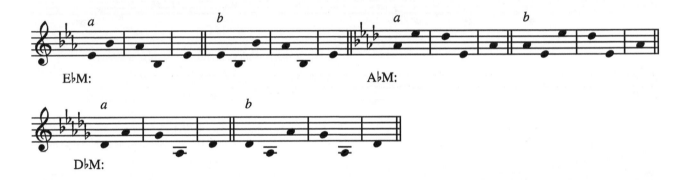

Follow the same principle of antiphonal singing with the next model. Letter "a" represents fragment 3 (Mozart's Horn Concerto, K. 447, first movement); "b" represents fragment 4 from the third movement of the same concerto.

Here is another model for antiphonal singing. Letter "a" corresponds with fragment 5 (from the second movement of the same horn concerto as fragments 3 and 4); "b" corresponds with fragment 6 from another Mozart horn concerto (K. 447, second movement).

This model follows the contour of fragment 7 (Haydn) and fragment 8 (Beethoven). Sing the model in all major keys.

The last three melodic fragments (9, 10, and 11) in the next section are further illustrations of the patterns already presented.

SECTION 2. Melodic Fragments in E♭ Major

8. Beethoven Piano Sonata op. 10, no. 1 (first movement)

Allegro molto e con brio

Beethoven Piano Concerto no. 5, op. 73 (second movement)

9.

Adagio un poco mosso ♩ = 60

10. Beethoven String Quartet op. 18, no. 3 (transposed)

Allegro ♩ = 120

11. Beethoven String Quartet op. 18, no. 4

Allegro ma non tanto ♩ = 84

SECTION 3. Creating a Coherent Melody

Return to section 2 and select two or three segments of melodic fragments that create a coherent melody. It may be necessary to change the meter and rhythm of certain segments, depending on your choice.

SECTION 4. Improvisation

The following vocalise pattern will be expanded in subsequent chapters and will eventually become the basis for improvisation exercises that modulate. For now, study the harmonic implications of this pattern and use it as a model for analyzing Mozart's use of V^7–I in excerpts from *The Magic Flute* (transposed to C). Improvise a melodic pattern in the spirit of one of the excerpts from *The Magic Flute*.

vocalise pattern

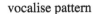

1. Mozart *The Magic Flute* no. 8 Finale (act I) Tamino (transposed)

Allegro

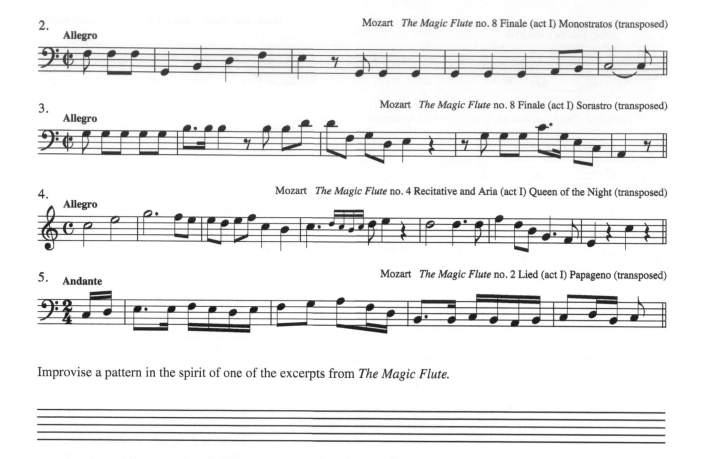

Improvise a pattern in the spirit of one of the excerpts from *The Magic Flute*.

C Melodies (Major and Minor): M6 and m6

SECTION 1. Melodies from Songs and Instrumental Works by Beethoven

The melodies in this section are from instrumental and vocal works by Beethoven.

2.

$$V^6_4 \quad \text{---} \quad {}^7_5{}_3$$

Beethoven   Three Sonatas, no. 3, II, Var. II, WoO 47

3.

$$V^6_4 \quad ^5_3$$

Beethoven   Three Sonatas, no.3, Var. VI, WoO 47

4.

$$V^6_4 \quad \text{---} \quad ^5_3$$

Beethoven   *Urians Reise um die Welt* (Urian's Journey Round the World), op. 52, no. 1

5. **In einer massigen geschwinden Bewegung mit einer komischen Art gesungen**

6.

Andante con moto

7.

Beethoven *Das Glück der freundschaft* (The Joy of Friendship), op. 88

Andante quasi allegretto

Beethoven *Der Mann von Wort* (A Man of His Word), op. 99 (transposed)

8. **Gemäss dem verschiedenen Ausdruck in den Versen piano und forte**

SECTION 2. Short Melodies by Bruce Benward

These short melodies will provide the opportunity for rapid reading of melodic patterns that are typical of music of the common practice period.

1.   2.

3.   4.

D Melodies (Major and Minor): M6 and m6

The melodies in this section are taken from instrumental works by George Friedrich Händel. The HWV numbers are from the reference manual of the *Händel-Handbuch* (vol. 3), published by Bärenreiter Kassel, Basel and London, 1986.

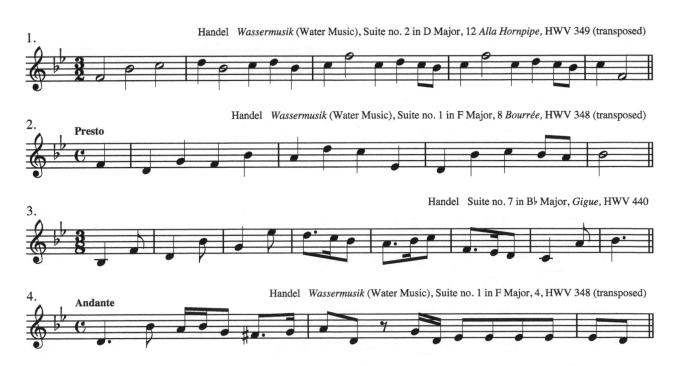

1. Handel *Wassermusik* (Water Music), Suite no. 2 in D Major, 12 *Alla Hornpipe*, HWV 349 (transposed)

2. Handel *Wassermusik* (Water Music), Suite no. 1 in F Major, 8 *Bourrée*, HWV 348 (transposed)

3. Handel   Suite no. 7 in B♭ Major, *Gigue*, HWV 440

4. Handel *Wassermusik* (Water Music), Suite no. 1 in F Major, 4, HWV 348 (transposed)

5. Handel Suite no. 1 in B♭ Major, *Menuet*, HWV 434 (transposed octave lower)

6. Handel Suite no. 9 in G Major, *Chaconne*, HWV 442 (transposed)

Fine

D.C.

7. Handel Suite no. 8 in G Major, *Gigue*, HWV 441

8. Handel Suite no. 3 in D Minor, Var. 4, HWV 428

9.

Handel Suite no. 5 in E Major, *Air*, "The Harmonious Blacksmith" HWV 430

10.

E Ensembles and Play + Sing

SECTION 1. Repertoire Using Treble and Bass Clefs

These excerpts are from works by Handel, Couperin, Haydn, and Bach.

Handel Suite no. 9 in G Major, Var. 62, HWV 442 (transposed)

1.

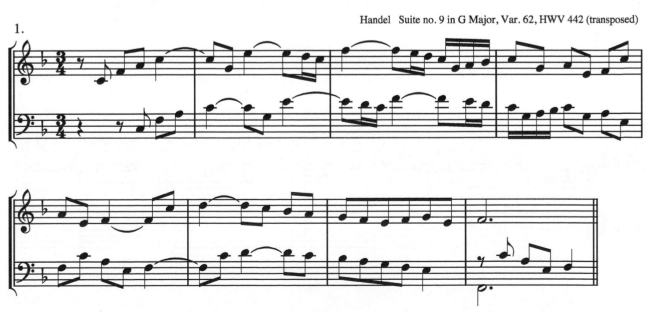

2.

Couperin *Les Moissonneurs* (The Reapers)

This is an interesting excerpt because, according to the directions, it may be sung forward and backward, then turned upside down and sung both forward and backward. The text translates freely: "You should dedicate yourself entirely to your art."

Haydn Die Zehn Gebote der Kunst (The Ten Commandments of Art), no. 1 "Du sollst dich ganz der Kunst weihen" (You should dedicate yourself entirely to your art)

3.

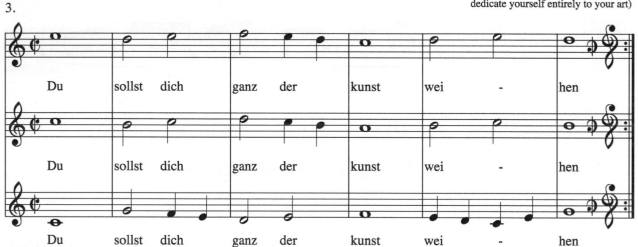

Du   sollst dich   ganz der   kunst   wei -   hen

Du   sollst dich   ganz der   kunst   wei -   hen

Du   sollst dich   ganz der   kunst   wei -   hen

Transpose this familiar melody down a major 2nd to G by reading the upper line in tenor clef (for these purposes, the fourth line is c", an 8ve higher than c') and the lower line in alto clef (for these purposes, the middle line is c, an 8ve lower than c').

4.

Bach Canon *In dulci jubilo* (In Sweet Jubilation), BWV 608

Inner voices omitted

SECTION 2. Repertoire Using C Clefs

William Billings "Africa" (1778)

SECTION 3. Play + Sing

Joseph Lanner *Pester Walzer*, op. 93, no. 1 (adapted and transposed from E minor)

2.

UNIT EIGHT

A Rhythm—Simple Meter: The Supertriplet

SECTION 1. Modules in Simple Meter

Begin by repeating each module several times. Then treat the successive modules as a continuous exercise.

SECTION 2. Phrases in Simple Meter with Supertriplets

6.

SECTION 3. Creating a Coherent Phrase in Simple Meter with Supertriplets

Return to section 1 and select three or four rhythm modules. Place the modules into a coherent four-measure phrase.

Write your solution on the following line:

B Diatonic Models and Melodic Fragments: m7 and M7

SECTION 1. Diatonic Models

The exercises in this section relate to the music of Verdi, Stravinsky, Wagner, Bach, and Beethoven with particular emphasis on the minor 7th (m7). The musical fragments that correspond with these exercises are quoted in section 2.

The first model (in minor) is related to the first melodic fragment (Bach); the second model (in major) is related to fragments 2 and 3 by Wagner. Sing the first model in keys a minor 3rd above (i.e., C, E♭, F♯), then sing the next model in keys a minor 3rd below (E♭, C, A, and so on).

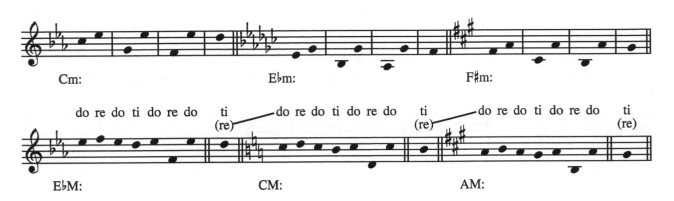

If you find it difficult to sing the second model in keys separated by a minor 3rd, the reason is that the melodic patterns combine to form a segment of the octatonic scale (i.e., a scale of alternating major and minor seconds). See the following model:

Only two models are necessary to introduce the major 7th (M7) from E♭ to D. These are preparatory materials for melodic fragments 5–7.

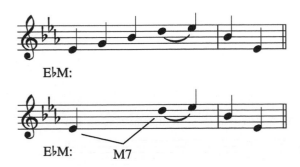

Only two models are necessary to introduce the major 7th (M7, from A♭ to G) as preparation for melodic fragments 8 and 9. The second model is almost the reverse of the first.

E♭M: M7   Cm: M7

These models are quite similar to the previous two, except that they are in minor keys. For those who want to emphasize relative relationships, C minor is provided; for those who prefer parallel relationships, E♭ minor is available. These models are in preparation for melodic fragments 10, 10a, 11, and 11a in the next section.

Cm:

E♭m:

SECTION 2. Melodic Fragments in C Minor and E♭ Major

Bach   Partita no. 6, *Gavotte* (transposed)

1.

Presto

Wagner *The Twilight of the Gods,* act III, scene 3 (transposed)

2.

Voriges Zeitmass, feierlich

Wagner *The Twilight of the Gods,* act III, scene 1 (transposed)

3.

Lebhaft

Wagner *The Twilight of the Gods,* act III, scene 2 (transposed)

4.

Feierlich

Verdi *Aida,* Act IV (transposed)

5.

Lento

6.

Stravinsky   *Petrushka* (transposed)

PETROUCHKA (Stravinsky) © Copyright 1912 by Hawkes & Son (London) Ltd. Copyright Renewed. Reprinted by permission of Boosey & Hawkes, Inc.

7.

Beethoven   Piano Sonata, op. 10, no. 3 (first movement—transposed)

8.

Bach   French Suite no. 6, *Allemande* (transposed)

9.

Bach   Partita no. 2, *Rondeau*

10.

Bach   French Suite no. 3, *Sarabande* (transposed)

11.

Bach   *Well-Tempered Clavier,* Book I, Fugue 10 (transposed)

12.

Bach   *Die Kunst der Fuge* (Art of Fugue), no. 9 (transposed)

13.

Bach   English Suite no. 5, *Gigue* (transposed)

SECTION 3. Creating a Coherent Melody

Return to section 2 and select two or three segments of melodic fragments that would create a coherent melody. It may be necessary to change the meter and rhythm of certain segments, depending on your choice.

SECTION 4. Improvisation

The following vocalise pattern that was introduced in unit 7-B-4 is now being expanded to include all inversions of the dominant seventh chord. Students should eventually memorize this expanded vocalise pattern.

Use the "expanded vocalise pattern" as the basis for an improvisation. Begin by taking one of the fragments from *The Magic Flute* in unit 7-B-4 and follow the "roadmap" of the expanded vocalise pattern. After you have established the linear harmonies for your improvisation, try to embellish these harmonies by dividing the quarter notes into eighth notes and by using as much stepwise motion as possible. Here is an example, using melody #2 as sung by Monostratos:

C Melodies (Major and Minor): m7

SECTION 1. Melodies from Operas by Verdi, Puccini, Handel, and Pergolesi

The melodies in this section are from operas by Verdi, Puccini, Handel, and Pergolesi.

5. **Andantino ingenuo** ♪ = 120   Puccini *Gianni Schicchi*, R–40 (transposed)
   dolce

   Lauretta

6.   Handel *Julius Caesar*, act I
   Largo

   Cleopatra

7.   Verdi *Attila*, act II, R–85
   Andante ♩ = 60

   Ezio

8.   Verdi *Attila*, act II, R–88
   Allegro giusto ♩ = 108

   Ezio

SECTION 2. Excerpts from Cantatas Written by J. S. Bach

The excerpts in this section are taken from the cantatas of J. S. Bach.

D Melodies (Major and Minor): m7

SECTION 1. Folk Songs and Instrumental Works

The first four melodies in this section are from folk song collections of the northern woods of the United States and of Haiti and emphasize some of the most complicated rhythm patterns presented thus far.

The juxtaposition of the Bruckner excerpts with those from the *Art of Fugue* later in this section, as well as in the subsequent part E, "Ensembles," gives evidence of Bruckner's homage to this monumental work by Bach.

"Driving Saw-Logs on the Plover" from *Lumbering Songs from the Northern Woods* by Edith Fowke, tunes transcribed by Norman Cazden. Published for the American Folklore Society by the University of Texas Press, Austin and London: Copyright 1970 by the American Folklore Society Memoir Series, Wm. Hugh Jansen, General Editor, vol. 55, 1970.

2.

"Save Your Money While You're Young" from *Lumbering Songs from the Northern Woods* by Edith Fowke, tunes transcribed by Norman Cazden. Published for the American Folklore Society by the University of Texas Press, Austin and London: Copyright 1970 by the American Folklore Society Memoir Series, Wm. Hugh Jansen, General Editor, vol. 55, 1970.

3.

Haiti "Fai Ogoun"

4.

Haiti "Ma fré"

11. Mendelssohn "Lord God of Abraham, Isaac and Israel" from *Elijah*, op. 70, no. 14 (adapted)

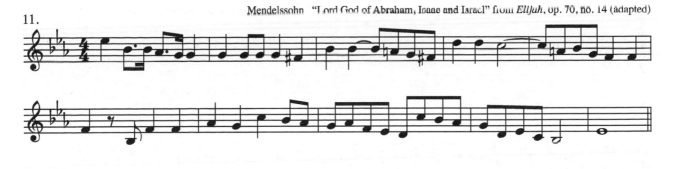

12. Sehr langsam
dolce
Bruckner Symphony no. 5, II

oboe

cello

13. Edward Elgar "Nimrod" from *Variations on an Original Theme for Orchestra ("Enigma")*, op. 36, meas. 1–9

Adagio

E Ensembles and Play + Sing

SECTION 1. Repertoire Using Treble and Bass Clefs

1. Adagio
Haydn *Gott im Herzen* (To Have God in One's Heart)

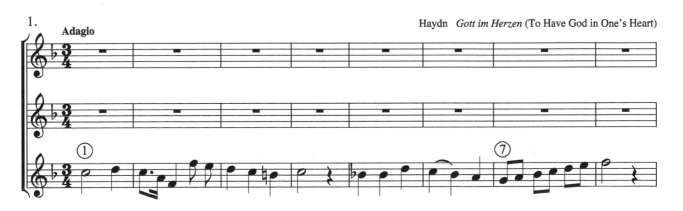

Bach *Die Kunst der Fuge* (Art of the Fugue), Contrapunctus V

2.

3.

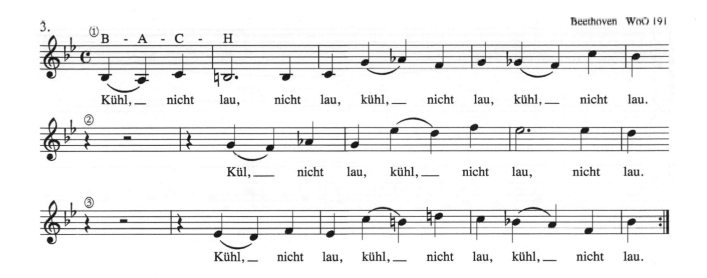

Beethoven WoO 191

(1) B - A - C - H
Kühl,— nicht lau, nicht lau, kühl,— nicht lau, kühl,— nicht lau.

(2)
Kül,— nicht lau, kühl,— nicht lau, nicht lau.

(3)
Kühl,— nicht lau, kühl,— nicht lau, kühl,— nicht lau.

SECTION 2. Repertoire Using C Clefs

Sergei Rachmaninov   No. 6, "Bogoroditse Devo" from *Vespers*, op. 37, meas. 1–13

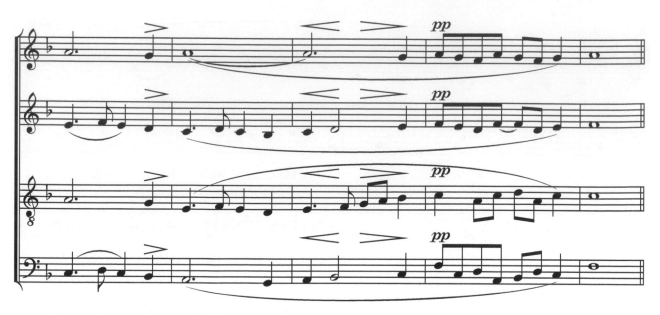

SECTION 3. Play + Sing

Edward Elgar   "Light out of Darkness" from *The Light of Life*, op. 29 (adapted and transposed)

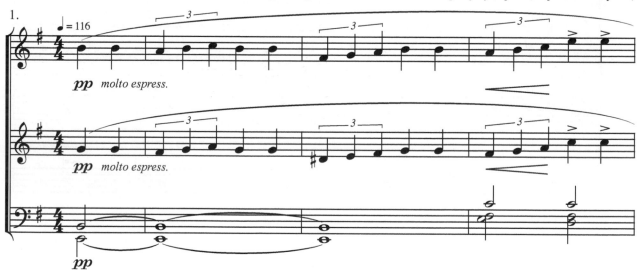

Leoš Janáček "Constitues eos principes," meas. 1–17 (adapted)

2.

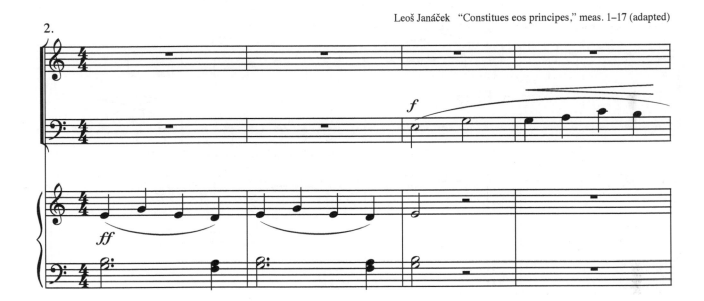

UNIT NINE

A Rhythm—Further Subdivisions of the Beat in Compound Meter and 3 against 2

SECTION 1. Modules in Compound Meter

Using rhythm syllables or a neutral syllable, sing each of the given modules. Begin by repeating each module several times, then treat the successive modules as a continuous exercise.

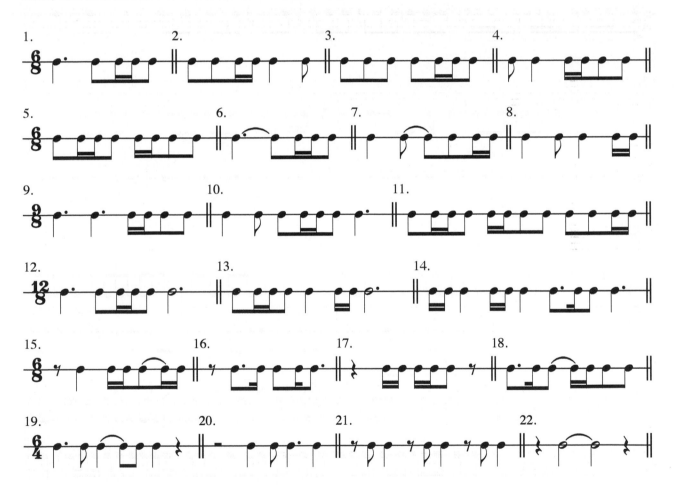

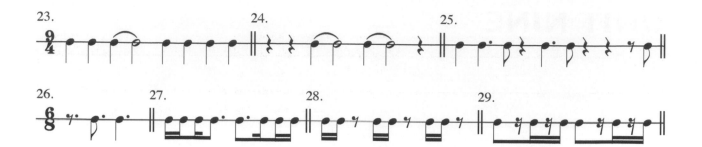

SECTION 2. Phrases with Triplets and 3 against 2

1. Rhythmic crescendo and decrescendo

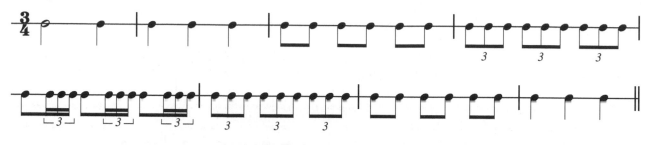

2.

3.

4. Rhythmic canon

5. Ostinato

SECTION 3. Creating a Coherent Phrase in Compound Meter

Using the rhythmic patterns provided in section 1, create a coherent four-measure phrase.

Write your solution on the following line:

B Diatonic Models and Melodic Fragments: A4 and d5

SECTION 1. Diatonic Models

The exercises in this section relate to the melodic fragments of Bach, Beethoven, and Mozart.

The following examples emphasize the resolution of the diminished 5th (d5; D♯–A) to the major 3rd (M3; E–G♯), as given in the following model:

Learning to sing the exercises derived from this excerpt will help you understand the intricacies of voice leading involved in the treatment of tritones. Most often, successive melodic tritones are harmonized by dominant 7th chords, moving sequentially downward by P5s. Sing the following model in all major keys, transposing to each new key by P5s down or P4s up, as shown in the following model:

Try the following accelerated method for traveling through the various keys.

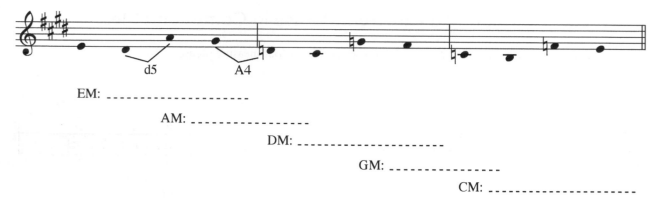

This model shows the resolution of the augmented 4th (A4; A–D♯) to the major 6th (M6; G–E) and is related to fragment 6.

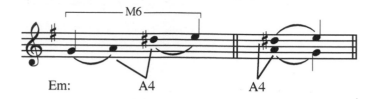

The next series of models relate to the Bach chorales in the next section.

7.

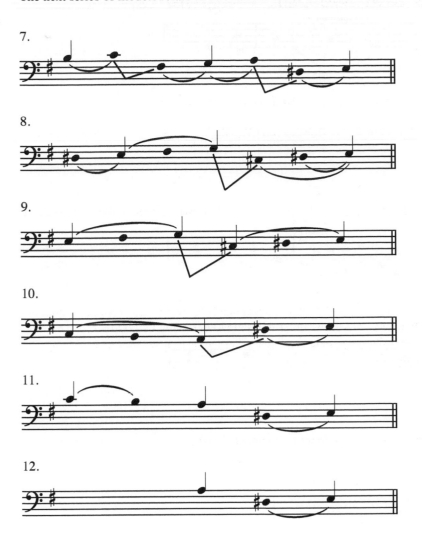

8.

9.

10.

11.

12.

SECTION 2. Melodic Fragments in E Major and E Minor

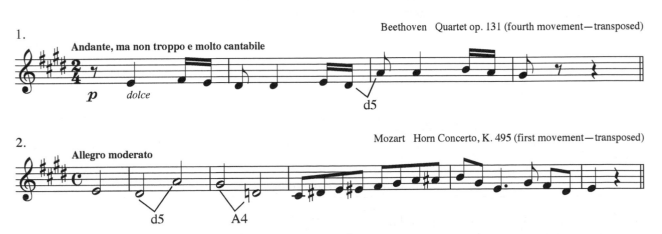

1.

Beethoven   Quartet op. 131 (fourth movement—transposed)

Andante, ma non troppo e molto cantabile

p   *dolce*

d5

2.

Mozart   Horn Concerto, K. 495 (first movement—transposed)

Allegro moderato

d5   A4

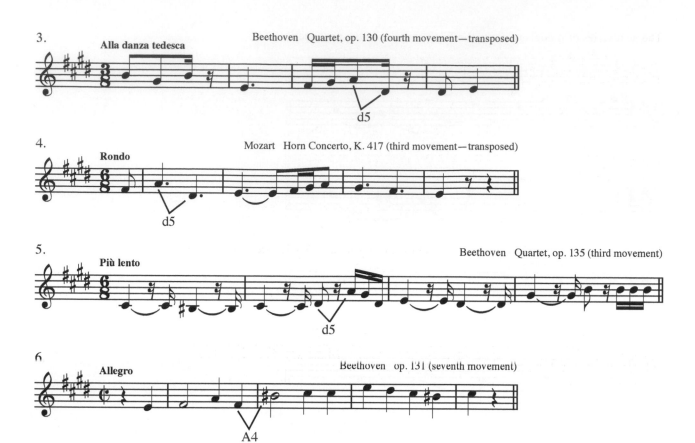

3.
Alla danza tedesca   Beethoven   Quartet, op. 130 (fourth movement—transposed)

d5

4.
Rondo   Mozart   Horn Concerto, K. 417 (third movement—transposed)

d5

5.
Più lento   Beethoven   Quartet, op. 135 (third movement)

d5

6
Allegro   Beethoven   op. 131 (seventh movement)

A4

For convenience, the Riemenschneider numbers are used to identify fragments 7–10.

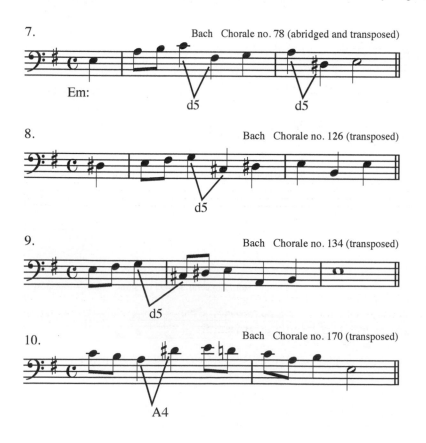

7.   Bach   Chorale no. 78 (abridged and transposed)

Em:

d5   d5

8.   Bach   Chorale no. 126 (transposed)

d5

9.   Bach   Chorale no. 134 (transposed)

d5

10.   Bach   Chorale no. 170 (transposed)

A4

11.

Bach   Chorale no. 178 (transposed)

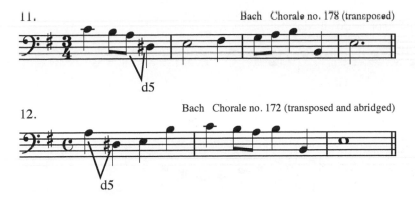

d5

12.

Bach   Chorale no. 172 (transposed and abridged)

d5

Supplemental fragments emphasizing secondary leading-tone [L.T.] functions.

Beethoven   Symphony no. 1, op. 21, I (m. 1–4 transposed from C major)

13.   **Adagio molto**   ♪ = 88

[L.T.] $\hat{4}$ L.T. $\hat{1}$ [L.T.] $\hat{5}$

EM:

d5   A4

Beethoven   Symphony no. 1, op. 21 (mm. 41–45 abridged and transposed)

14.   **Allegro con brio**   ♩ = 112

L.T. $\hat{1}$ [L.T.] $\hat{2}$ [L.T.] $\hat{3}$ [L.T.] $\hat{4}$ [L.T.] $\hat{5}$

EM:

SECTION 3.   Creating a Coherent Melody

Return to section 2 and select two or three segments of melodic fragments that create a coherent melody. It may be necessary to change the meter and rhythm of certain segments, depending on your choice.

SECTION 4.   Improvisation

The vocalise pattern that was introduced in unit 7-B-4 is now extended to include a modulatory pattern. Be mindful of the thin line that exists between modulation and tonicization. This pattern can be shaped to produce a modulation or a tonicization, depending on the context that you establish in your improvisation.

The first exercise is structured according to the basic vocalise pattern; the second one is more free to encourage you to create your own modulatory improvisation.

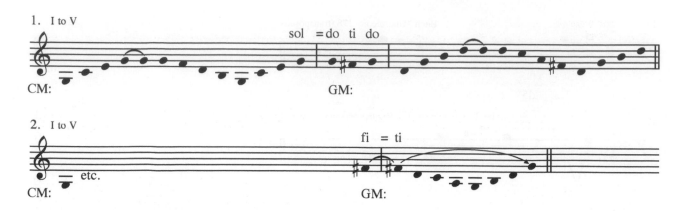

1. I to V

sol = do ti do

CM: GM:

2. I to V

fi = ti

etc.

CM: GM:

The following work is a strophic song by Schubert. Within the framework of G major, Schubert raises scale-degree 4 (from C♮ to C♯), establishing a modulation from I to V. This is the same tonal plan that you experienced in the modulatory patterns above. In m. 11, Schubert returns to G major by lowering C♯ to C♮.

Schubert *Heidenröslein* (Wild Rose), D. 257

C Melodies (Major): Chromatic Alterations, Modulating, and Nonmodulating

The melodies in this section are excerpts from the Mozart song literature. These excerpts were transposed to the key of C major for ease in seeing and hearing notes outside the diatonic framework. Examples include alterations of the following scale degrees: 4 (F♯), 2 (D♯), 5 (G♯), and 1 (C♯). These exercises are designed to assist you with the Mozart songs in the next part of this unit.

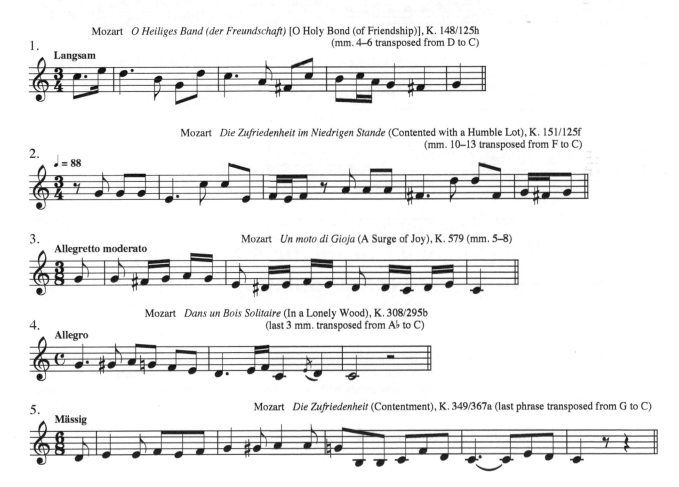

6. **Traurig, doch gelassen**
Mozart *An die Einsamkeit* (In Solitude), K. 391/340b (mm. 7–13 transposed from B♭ to C)

7. **Larghetto**
Mozart *Gesellenreise (Freimaurerlied)* [Life's Journey (Song of the Freemason)], K. 468
(mm. 1–2 transposed from B♭ to C)

8. ♩ = 88
Mozart *Des kleinen Friedrichs Geburtstag* (Little Frederick's Birthday), K. 529
(last 2 mm. transposed from F to C)

9. **Andante**
Mozart *Zum Schluss* (At the End), K. 484 (last phrase transposed from G to C)

10. ♩. = 66
Mozart *Die Verschweigung* (Discretion), K. 518 (mm. 10–17 transposed from F to C)

D Melodies (Major): Chromatic Alterations, Modulating, and Nonmodulating

SECTION 1. Mozart Songs

Not all of the melodies contain modulations, but in addition to the possibility of modulations, melodies in this part may also include chromatic alterations because of one or another of the following: (1) accompaniments with secondary dominant or leading-tone harmonies; (2) accompaniments with other chromatic harmonies, such as borrowed chords, augmented 6ths, and Neapolitan 6ths; and (3) chromatic nonharmonic tones.

Your instructor will provide directions for the use of syllables or numbers as they relate to the sources of alteration.

4.

5.

Mozart *Sehnsucht nach dem Frülinge* (Longing for Spring), K. 596 (transposed)

*See unit 13, part B, for d4.

6.

Mozart *Im Frühlingsanfang* (At Spring's Outset), K. 597

Mozart *An Chloe* (To Chloe, 2nd half of song), K. 524 (transposed)

7. **Allegretto**

Mozart *Un moto di Gioja* (A Surge of Joy, 2nd half of song), K. 579 (abridged)

8. **Allegretto moderato**

Mozart *Die Verschweigung* (Discretion), K. 518

9. **No tempo given**

Mozart *Abendempfindung* (Evening Song, 2nd half of song), K. 523

10.

Andante

SECTION 2. Melodies from Operas by Rameau

This section includes three melodies from eighteenth-century opera. The first two solo excerpts are sung by Émilie in Rameau's opera-ballet *Les Indes galants* (The Courtly Indies), first performed on August 23, 1735. The third excerpt is sung by Télaïre in *Castor et Pollux.*

1.   Rameau *Les Indes galantes* (The Courtly Indies) Émilie

Tempête

Reprinted by arrangement with Broude Brothers Limited.

2. **Tempête**

Reprinted by arrangement with Broude Brothers Limited.

3. **Très lent**

FINE

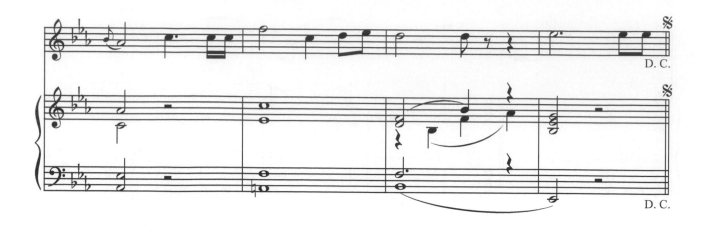

E Ensembles and Play + Sing

SECTION 1. Repertoire Using Treble and Bass Clefs

The first example is the eighth canon from a group of ten written by Haydn, titled *Die Heiligen Zehn Gebote als Canons* (The Ten Commandments).

Joseph Haydn Werke XXXI, Die heiligen Zehn Gebote, no. 8. © 1959 by G. Henle Verlag, Muenchen, used by permission.

2.

Bach *Wer hat dich so geschlagen* (Who Was It, Lord, Did Smite Thee) from *St. Matthew Passion*, BWV 244

SECTION 2. Repertoire Using C Clefs

Mozart *Selig, selig, alle, alle* [Blessed, Blessed All, All (Who Sleep in the Lord)] Canon for 2 Voices, K. 230

Bach *Ich will hier bei dir stehen* (I Stand Here Close Beside Thee) from *St. Matthew Passion*, BWV 244

2.

SECTION 3. Play + Sing

1.

Saint-Saëns "Tortues" (Tortoises) from *La Carnaval des Animaux* (Carnival of the Animals) (adapted)

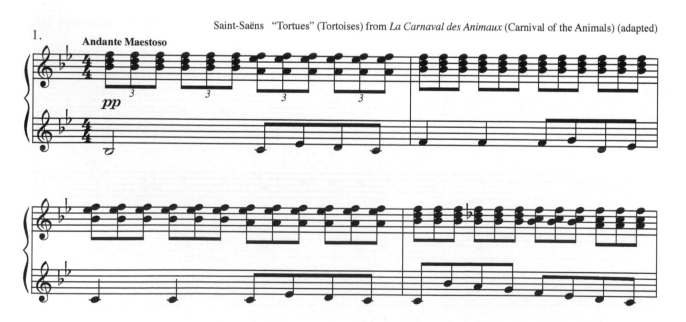

Brahms   Intermezzo in A minor, op. 116, no. 2

2.

3.

UNIT TEN

A   Rhythm—Changing Meter with Triplets and Aligned and Displaced Hemiolas

Use the conducting patterns shown below, if your instructor recommends you do so.

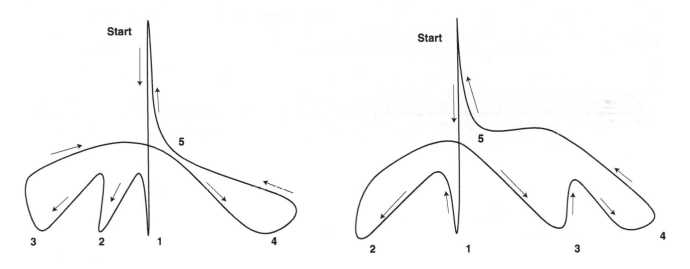

SECTION 1. Modules

Using rhythm syllables or a neutral syllable, sing each of the given modules. Begin by repeating each module several times, then treat the successive modules as a continuous exercise.

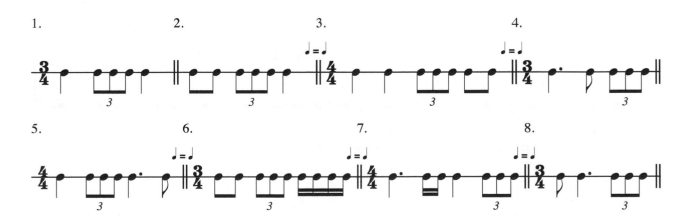

SECTION 2. Phrases Using Aligned and Displaced Hemiolas

The following rhythmic frameworks are adapted from waltzes by Lanner and Strauss Sr.

1. Aligned

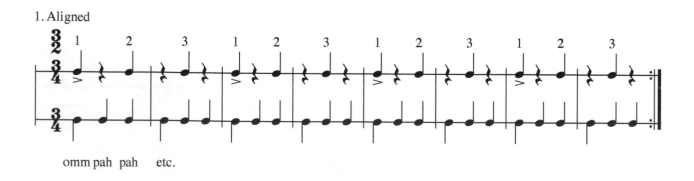

omm pah pah   etc.

2. Displaced by one beat (see 10E3-1)

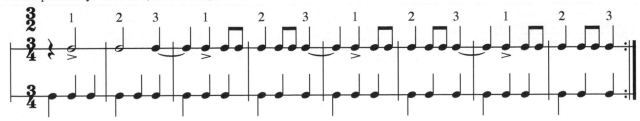

3. Displaced by two beats (see 10E3-2)

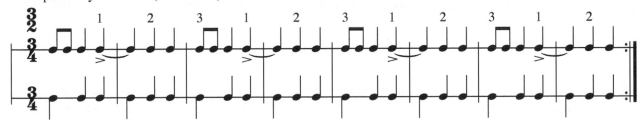

SECTION 3. Creating a Coherent Phrase in Simple Meter

Using rhythmic patterns provided in section 1, create a coherent four-measure phrase.

Write your solution on the following line:

B Diatonic and Chromatic Models and Melodic Fragments: A4 and d5

SECTION 1. Diatonic and Chromatic Models

As in the previous unit, these exercises focus on the tritone. In this unit, however, the models are based on fragments by a different set of composers: Wagner, Stravinsky, Franck, Mussorgsky, Debussy, Schubert, and Barber. Many of these models are extracted from highly chromatic textures, but the exercises themselves are mostly diatonic. Often the notes of resolution associated with the tritone, in traditional terms, are partially or fully absent in some exercises. The unifying thread that runs throughout part B of this unit is the pitch-specific nature of the tritone D♯–A. The one exception occurs in melodic fragments 9–11, where the transposition to relative minor changes D♯–A to F♯–C.

Follow the same procedure as in previous units. Sing the following model in all major keys.

EM: AM: DM:

The following table indicates how the models (in this section) relate to the fragments in section 2.

Models	Fragments
1 & 2	1 & 2
3	3
4	2
5	5
6	4
7	6
8	7
9	8
10	9
11	10

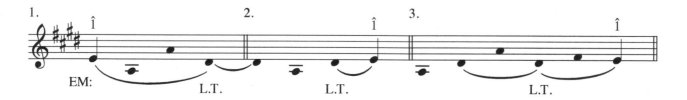

The following model shows how a tritone (A–D♯) is filled in with a M3 (A–C♯) and a M2 (C♯–D♯). The next model shows how the same tritone is approached by a M2 (B–A) and left by a M3 (D♯–B).

The next three models feature a tritone that is not filled in.

These models relate to fragments 9, 10, and 11 of the next section.

SECTION 2. Melodic Fragments in E Major and E Minor

Wagner *Götterdämmerung* (The Twilight of the Gods), act III (transposed)

1.

d5

2.

Barber "I Hear an Army" (transposed)

A4   A4

I HEAR AN ARMY from *Three Songs*, op. 10. By Samuel Barber. Copyright © 1939 (Renewed) by G. Schirmer, Inc. (ASCAP) International Copyright Secured. All Rights Reserved. Reprinted by Permission.

3.

Stravinsky *Petroushka*, (transposed)

A4   d5   d5

PETROUCHKA (Stravinsky) © Copyright 1912 by Hawkes & Son (London) Ltd. Copyright Renewed. Reprinted by permission of Boosey & Hawkes, Inc.

4.

Wagner *Götterdämmerung*, act III, scene iii

A4   A4

5.

Franck   Violin Sonata for Violin and Piano (second movement—transposed)

A4

Debussy *Des femmes de Paris* (The Dames of Paris),
from *Three Ballads of François Villon*, III (transposed)

6.

A4

7.

Wagner *Götterdämmerung*, act III, scene iii (transposed)

8. **Andante tranquillo**

Mussorgsky *Boris Godunov*, act I, scene i (transposed)

9. **Langsam**

Schubert *Ihr Bild (Her Picture)* (transposed)

10. **Moderato**

Barber "Rain Has Fallen" (transposed)

SECTION 3. Creating a Coherent Melody

Return to section 2 and select two or three segments of melodic fragments that create a coherent melody. It may be necessary to change the meter and rhythm of certain segments, depending on your choice.

SECTION 4. Improvisation

Refer to unit 9-B-4 if you have questions about "modulatory patterns" from tonic to dominant in major keys. In this section, we will focus on modulatory patterns from tonic to mediant in minor keys.

Modulatory patterns from C minor to E-flat major

1. i to III

2. i to III

Cm: E♭M:

In the first phrase of the following work, Beethoven moves from A minor to C major. This is the same tonal plan that you experienced in the modulatory patterns above. The second phrase begins in C major and quickly moves back to A minor.

Beethoven Symphony No. 7 (second movement)

3.   **Allegretto** ♩ = 76.

C Melodies with Chromatic Alterations

This section contains 11 melodies by the Schumanns. Numbers 1–5 are by Clara Schumann; numbers 6–11 are by Robert Schumann.

The first two melodies are excerpts from Clara Schumann's Three songs, opus 12 (text by F. Rückert) [attributed to Clara Schumann within Robert Schumann's Liebesfrühling ("Spring of Love," op. 37, nos. 2 and 11)].

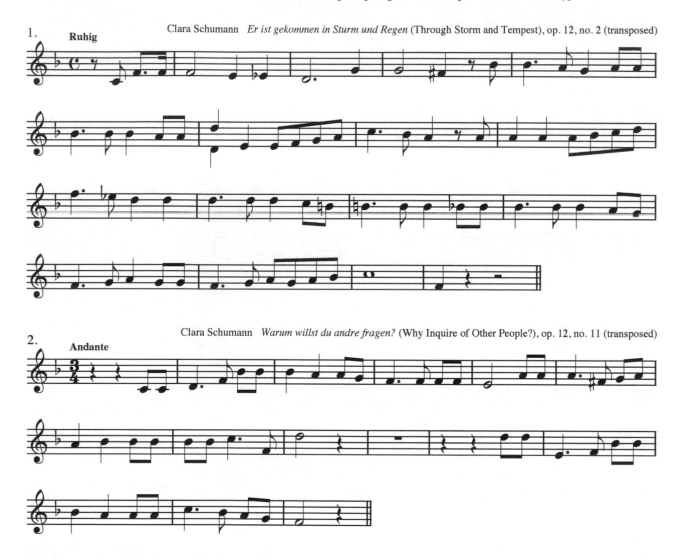

1.
Ruhig
Clara Schumann *Er ist gekommen in Sturm und Regen* (Through Storm and Tempest), op. 12, no. 2 (transposed)

2.
Andante
Clara Schumann *Warum willst du andre fragen?* (Why Inquire of Other People?), op. 12, no. 11 (transposed)

Melodies 1–2 © 1990 by Breitkopf & Härtel, Wiesbaden.

Here are two other settings by Clara Schumann.

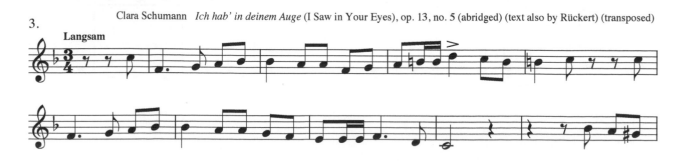

3.
Langsam
Clara Schumann *Ich hab' in deinem Auge* (I Saw in Your Eyes), op. 13, no. 5 (abridged) (text also by Rückert) (transposed)

Clara Schumann *Was weinst du, Blümlein* (Why Are You Weeping, Little Flower), op. 23, no. 1 (abridged) (text by Rollett) (transposed)

4.

Allegretto

rit. *a tempo*

mf

Melodies 3–4 © 1990 by Breitkopf & Härtel, Wiesbaden.

Clara Schumann Piano Trio (mm. 265–275)

5. **Allegro moderato**

animato

Breitkopf & Härtel, Wiesbaden. Used by permission.

Robert Schumann *Widmung* (Dedication), op. 25, no. 1 (transposed)

6. **Innig, lebhaft**

7. Robert Schumann *Was soll ich sagen* (What Shall I Say), op. 27, no. 3

8. Robert Schumann *Der Hidalgo* (The Hidalgo), op. 30, no. 3 (transposed) (abridged)

9. Robert Schumann *Stirb, Lieb' und Freud!* (Death, Love and Joy), op. 35, no. 2

10. **Sehr langsam**

Robert Schumann *Nichts Schöneres* (Nothing More Beautiful), op. 36, no. 3 (transposed) (abridged)

11. **Einfach, innig**

D Melodies with Chromatic Alterations

All the melodies in this section are taken from works by Felix Mendelssohn (*Songs Without Words*). All include alterations due to one or another of the following: (a) accompaniments with secondary-dominant or leading-tone harmonies; (b) accompaniments with other chromatic harmonies such as borrowed chords, augmented 6ths, Neapolitan 6ths, and so on; (c) fully established modulations; and (d) chromatic nonharmonic tones. Your instructor will provide directions for the use of syllables or numbers as they relate to the sources of alteration listed above.

Mendelssohn *Consolation*, op. 30, no. 3 (abridged)

1.

7. **Andante sostenuto**

Mendelssohn *Elegy*, op. 85, no. 4 (abridged) (transposed)

8. **Adagio**

Mendelssohn *Retrospection*, op. 102, no. 2 (abridged) (transposed)

9. **Presto**

Mendelssohn *Tarantella*, op. 102, no. 3 (abridged) (transposed)

Fine

D.C. al Fine

10.   Mendelssohn *Belief*, op. 102, no. 6 (abridged)

E   Ensembles and Play + Sing

SECTION 1.   Repertoire Using Treble and Bass Clefs

1.   Beethoven *Freundschaft* (Friendship), Canon for Three Voices, WoO 164

2.   G. P. Telemann *Fuga 2* (Fugue)

SECTION 2. Repertoire Using C Clefs

Haydn's *Thy Voice O Harmony* is a *cancrizans canon* in three voices—also known as a "crab canon"—also known as a retrograde canon. Can you find which line or lines sing the melody backward?

Haydn *Thy Voice O Harmony*

Joseph Haydn Werke XXXI, Weltlichen Kanons, no. 46. © 1959 by G. Henle Verlag, Muenchen, used by permission.

SECTION 3. Play + Sing

1.

Johann Strauss Sr. *Mittel gegen den Schlaf* (Remedy for Sleep) op. 65 (adapted)

Joseph Lanner *Musikvereins-Tänze* (Dances of the Music Society) op. 45 (adapted)

UNIT ELEVEN

A Rhythm—Subdivisions of the Beat into Eight Parts

SECTION 1. Modules

Begin by repeating each module several times. Then treat the successive modules as a continuous exercise.

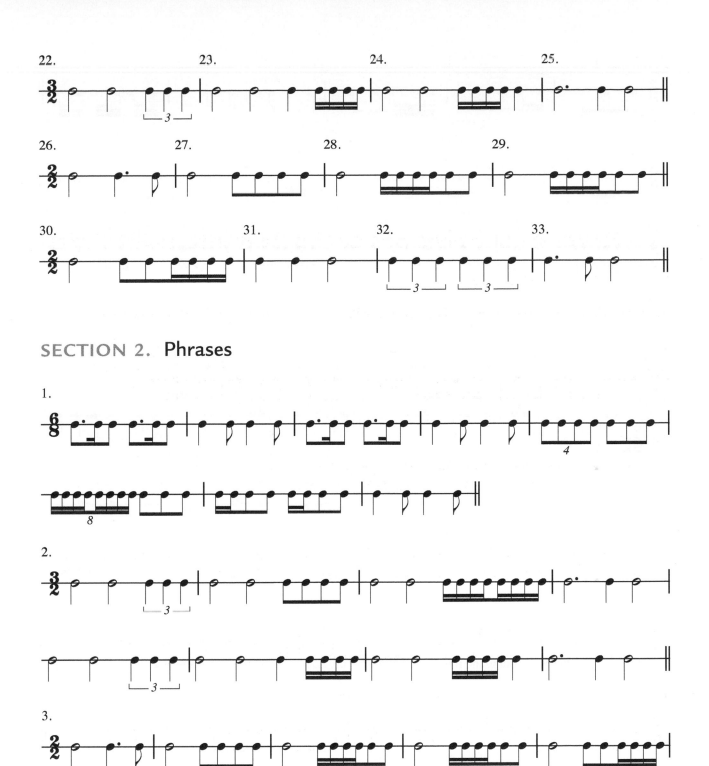

SECTION 2. Phrases

4.

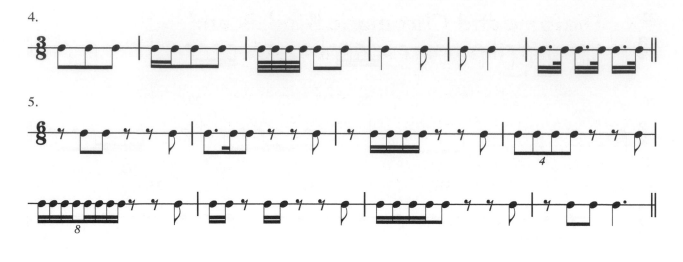

5.

6.

Rhythmic skeleton of Dvorák's Symphony no. 9, third movement (see E3, example 2)

Molto vivace ♩. = 80

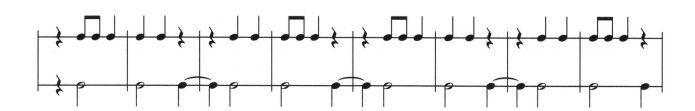

SECTION 3. Creating a Coherent Phrase

Using rhythmic patterns in compound meter from section 1, create a coherent four-measure phrase.

Write your solution on the following line:

B Diatonic and Chromatic Models and Melodic Fragments: d7 and A2

SECTION 1. Diatonic and Chromatic Models

The models in this section relate to the fragments in the next section as follows:

Models	Fragments
1	1
2	2
3	3, 4, 5, 6
4	5
5	7a,b,c,d
6	7a,b,c,d
7	7a,b,c,d
8a	8
8b	8
9	11, 12, 13, 14
10	11, 12, 13, 14, 15

MODELS 1–4

All the d7s in these models extend from B♮ up to A♭ or from A♭ down to B♮.

Follow the same procedures as in previous units. For extra practice, sing the first model in all minor keys, transposing to each new key by P5s down or P4s up (see model below). Because the d7 is so neatly framed by the tonic triad, these patterns are excellent for "tossing," i.e., for singing in alternation between two groups, as in previous units.

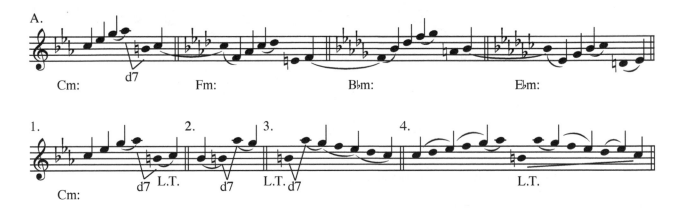

MODELS 5–7

Models 5–7 outline the basic motives of the opening notes of Beethoven's Quartet op. 133 (The Grand Fugue). Melodic fragments 7a, b, c, and d are from the same quartet. Memorize model 7 so you can "hear" these fragments with your eyes when you reach section 2.

5.   6.   7.

Cm: M2   M2   d7   m6   M6

MODEL 8

This model focuses on the A2 (from B♮ down to A♭ or from A♭ up to B♮). This A2 has the same pitches as the d7s in models 1–4.

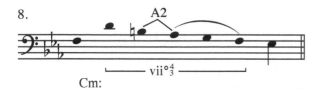

8.

A2

vii°$_3^4$

Cm:

MODELS 9–10

The leading-tone 7th chord, in root position, outlines the d7 chord and emphasizes the resulting symmetry (m3s or their enharmonic equivalent).

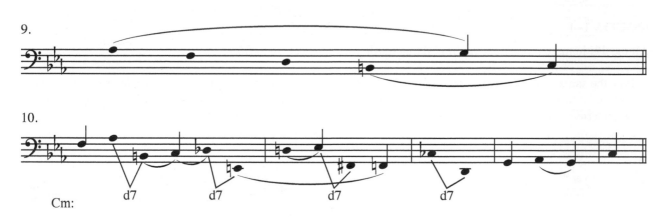

9.

10.

Cm: d7   d7   d7   d7

SECTION 2. Melodic Fragments in C Minor

Bach   *Musikalisches Opfer* (The Musical Offering)

1.

Lento

d7

Beethoven   String Quartet op. 132, I (transposed)

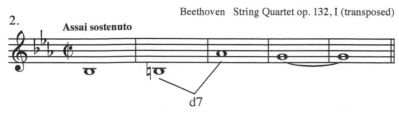

2.

Assai sostenuto

d7

3.

Beethoven   String Quartet op. 133, I (transposed)

Allegro molto e con brio

d7

4.

Bach   Two-Part Invention no. 4 (transposed)

Andante

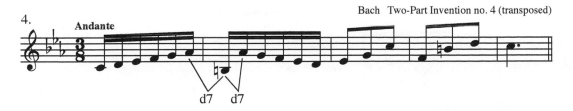

d7   d7

5.

Bach   Three-Part Invention no. 2 (transposed)

Andante

d7 d7

6.

Bach   Two-Part Invention no. 2

Moderato

d7

7a.

Beethoven   String Quartet op. 133, First Section (transposed)

Allegro

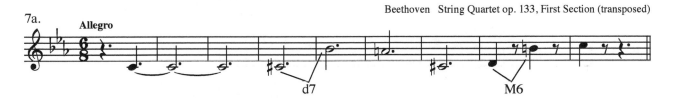

d7   M6

7b.

Beethoven   String Quartet op. 133, First Section (transposed)

Allegro

d7   M6

7c.

Beethoven   String Quartet op. 133, First Section (transposed)

Meno mosso e moderato

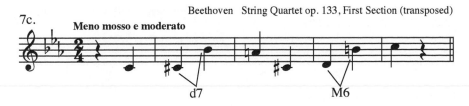

d7   M6

7d.

Beethoven   String Quartet op. 133, First Section (transposed)

8.
Haydn   Piano Sonata XVI: 16 (transposed)
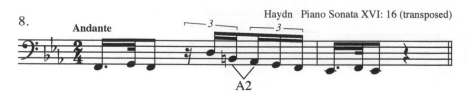

9.
Haydn   Piano Sonata XVI: 12 II (transposed)

10.
Haydn   Song *Dir nah ich mich, nah mich dem Throne* (I Approach You, I Approach the Throne) (transposed)

11.
Wagner   *Götterdämmerung*, act III, scene ii (transposed)

12.
Wagner   *Götterdämmerung*, act III, scene i (transposed)

13.
Wagner   *Götterdämmerung*, act III, scene i (transposed)

14.

15.

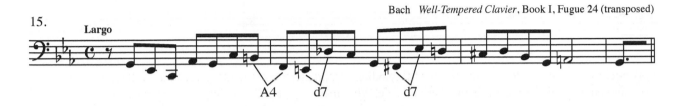

SECTION 3. Creating a Coherent Melody

Return to section 2 and select two or three segments of melodic fragments that create a coherent melody. It may be necessary to change the meter and rhythm of certain segments depending on your choice.

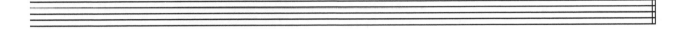

SECTION 4. Improvisation

The following parodies should help you to differentiate between minor-type modes (dorian, aeolian, and phrygian) and major-type modes (mixolydian, ionian, and lydian). Try to memorize these parodies so that you will be able to identify the characteristic intervallic patterns for each of the modes.

Major-type parodies

1. Ionian (major scale)

2. Mixolydian

3. Lydian

Minor-type parodies

4. Aeolian (natural minor scale)

5. Dorian

6. Phrygian

Folk music of the British Isles often uses the Mixylodian or Dorian modes. The following tune, well known among fiddlers and penny whistlers, is set in the Dorian mode. After memorizing the tune, improvise new jig melodies over the chord changes of the first eight-measure phrase.

Traditional Irish jig "Swallowtail"

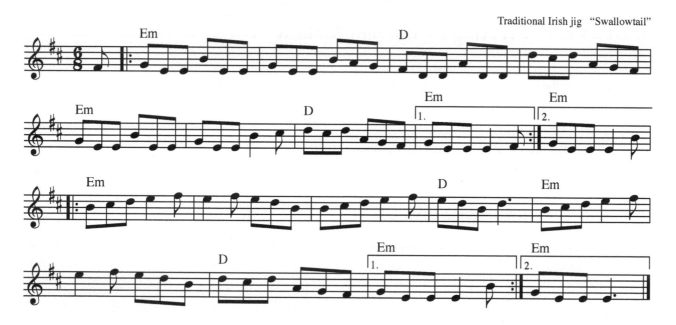

C Melodies with Modal Characteristics

1. Allegro

Stravinsky *Timlimbom* from *Histoire pour enfants* (Three Tales for Children), no. 1 (abridged)

Timlimbom from *Histoire pour enfants* (Three Tales for Children), no. 1. Masters Music Publications, Inc., Publisher in the U.S.A.

"Derreen Day" from *Songs of the Irish*

2.

Andante

From *Songs of the Irish* by Donal O'Sullivan. Published by the Mercier Press, Cork, Ireland. Used by permission.

The *Vocalise étude* by Gabriel Fauré is without text.

Chopin Mazurka op. 68, no. 3 (transposed)

3.

Poco più vivo

English sea shanty "Drunken Sailor"

4.

5.   American folk song "Old Joe Clark"

6.   Machaut "Douce dame jolie" (Sweet Lovely Lady), Medieval virelai

7.   Wizlaw von Rügen "Loybere risen" (Dark Leaves Are Flying), Medieval Minnesang

8.   Jewish Lullaby "Lulla Lulla"

Traditional Irish folk song   "She Moved through the Fair"

9.

Stravinsky   *Chanson pour compter* (Counting Song), from *Quatre Chants Russes* (Four Russian Songs), no. 2 (abridged)

10.

♩ = 168

Chanson pour compter (Counting Song) by Igor Stravinsky, from *Quartre Chants Russes* (Four Russian Songs), no. 2. Masters Music Publications, Inc., Publisher in the U.S.A.

"Farewell to Carraig An Éide" from *Songs of the Irish*

11.

Poco pesante

From *Songs of the Irish* by Donal O'Sullivan. Published by Mercier Press, Cork, Ireland. Used by permission.

12.

"'Tis the Last Rose of Summer" *Air: Groves of Blarney*, from Holden (modified by Moore)

D More Melodies

SECTION 1. Sacred Melodies with Modal Characteristics

Iordansky *Deux mélodies hébraïques* (Two Hebraic Melodies), 1

1. **Moderato**

"Como poden" (Let Us Sing) from *Cantigas de Santa Maria* (Songs of Saint Mary)

2.

3. Berlioz *Dignare Domine* (Prayer), *Te Deum*

Moderato quasi andantino

4. *Hymn to St. Thomas Aquinas* Gregorian Chant

5. *In Paradisum* (Into Paradise)   Gregorian Chant

6. *Jesu dulcis memoria* (The Hymn of St. Bernard)   from Mr. Southwell

7. Funeral Cry   Galway, August 28th, 1840

    Agitato

8. Christmas Carol or Hymn (as sung in the county of Galway)   from Mrs. Close

    Lento (♩ = 69)

9. Irish Hymn Sung on the Dedication of a Chapel, Co. of Londonderry

    Andante

SECTION 2. Songs by Brahms

1. Sehr lebhaft — Brahms *Tambourliedchen* (The Little Drummer's Song), op. 69, no. 5 (abridged and transposed)

2. Etwas bewegt — Brahms *Therese,* op. 86, no. 1 (abridged)

3. Bewegt und heimlich — Brahms *Spannung* (Tension), op. 84, no. 5 (abridged and transposed)

4. Andante moderato — Brahms *Anklänge* (Reminiscences), op. 7, no. 3 (abridged)

Brahms *So willst du des Armen dich gnädig erbarmen?* ('Tis Not Then a Dream?), from *Romanzen aus Magelone* (Romances from Magelone), op. 33, no. 5 (abridged and transposed)

5.

Allegro

Brahms *Über die Heide* (Over the Heath), op. 86, no. 4 (abridged)

6. **Ziemlich langsam, gehend**

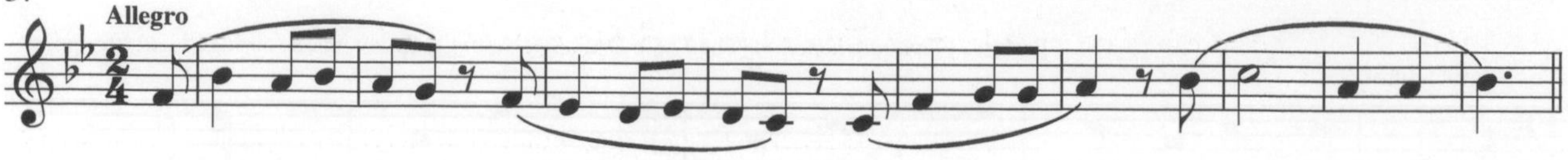

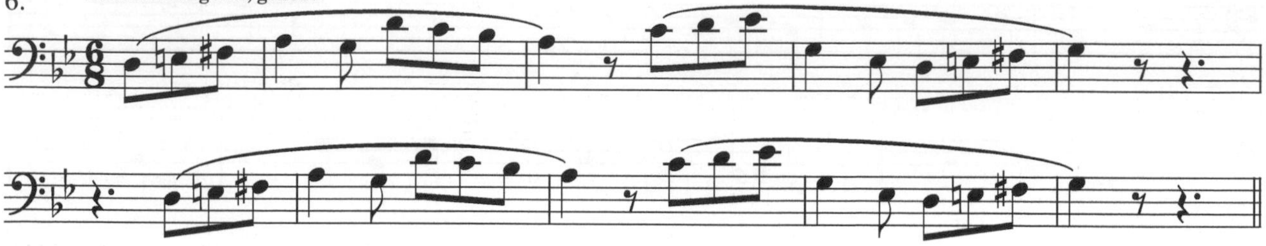

7. **Lebhaft**

Brahms *Der Jäger* (The Huntsman), op. 95, no. 4 (abridged and transposed)

Brahms *Trennung* (Separation), op. 97, no. 6 (abridged and transposed)

8.

Anmutig bewegt

9. **Nicht zu langsam und mit Anmut**

Brahms *An den Mond* (To the Moon), op. 71, no. 2 (abridged)

10.

Brahms *Spanisches Lied* (Spanish Song), op. 6, no. 1 (abridged)

Allegretto

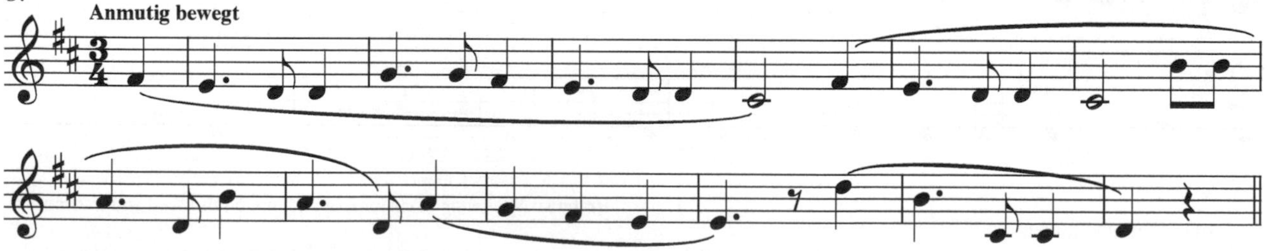

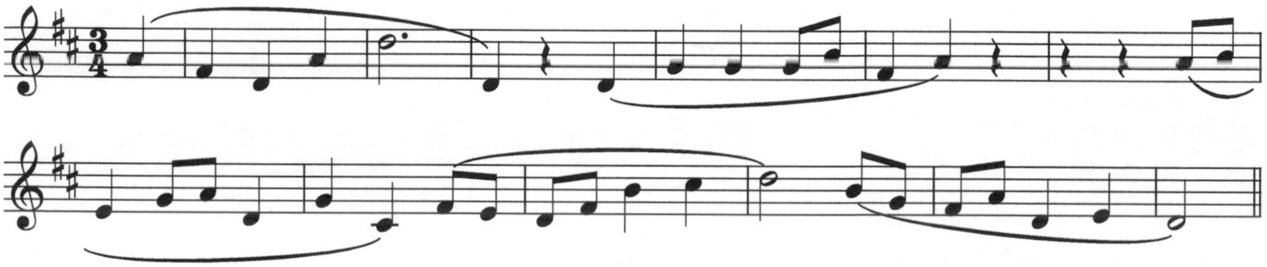

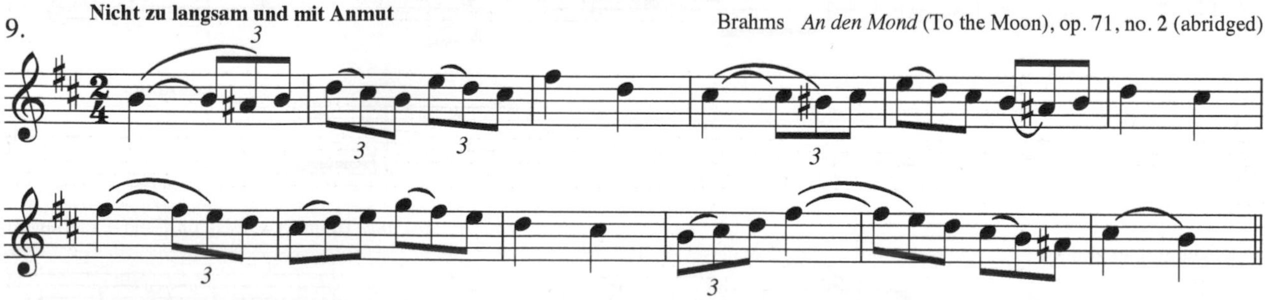

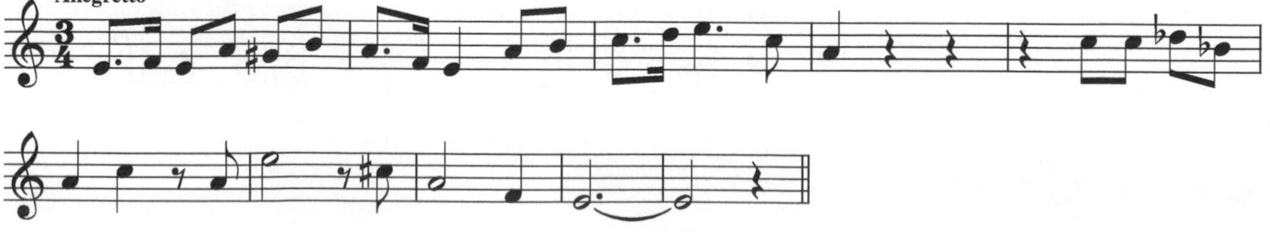

E Ensembles and Play + Sing

SECTION 1. Repertoire Using Treble and Bass Clefs

1.

Brahms   Thirteen Canons op. 113, 1 *Göttlicher Morpheus* (Divine Morpheus) (Text: Goethe)

Andante espressivo

Printed with the friendly permission of Breitkopf & Härtel, Wiesbaden.

Brahms   Thirteen Canons op. 113, **2** *Grausam erweiset sich Amor an mir* (Amor Proves to Be So Cruel) (Text: Goethe)

2.

Andante con moto

Printed with the friendly permission of Breitkopf & Härtel, Wiesbaden.

Brahms Thirteen Canons, op. 113, 3 *Sitzt a schöns Vögerl aufm Dannabaum* (There Sits a Lovely Bird upon the Christmas Tree)
(Text: traditional Austrian in A. von Kretzschmer and A.W. von Zuccalmaglio: German folksong)

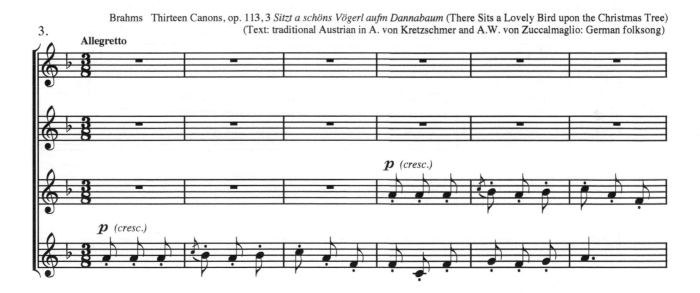

Printed with the friendly permission of Breitkopf & Härtel, Wiesbaden.

The B♭ clarinet sounds a M2 lower than written. Use the tenor clef to indicate c″ in singing the transposition. Check your accuracy in the reading of the clarinet part with the harp part. Both lines sound in unison.

Mahler   *Der Abschied* (The Farewell), from *Das Lied von der Erde* (Song of the Earth)

Wohl - laut - durch das Dun - kel

Die Blu - men blass - en im Däm - mer - schein.

SECTION 2. Repertoire Using C Clefs

Here we have the canon without realization (realization is found in subsequent example). In the dedication copy, Bach added the note, "Ascendenteque Modulatione ascendat Gloria Regis" (And may the glory of the King rise with the rising modulation); quoted from the Dover edition.

1.

Bach *Musikalisches Opfer* (The Musical Offering)

Bach *The Musical Offering*, Canon no. 5 *Per tonos** realization by J. P. Kirnberger; translated as (Ascending through the keys) in the Dover edition.

Bach *Musikalisches Opfer* (The Musical Offering)

2.

SECTION 3. Play + Sing

Bizet "Carillon" from *L'Arlésienne* (adapted, abridged, and transposed)

Dvoràk Symphony no. 9 (third movement) (adapted and abridged)

2.

Molto vivace ♩. = 80

UNIT TWELVE

A Rhythm—The Quartolet

SECTION 1. Modules

Begin by repeating each module several times. Then treat the successive modules as a continuous exercise.

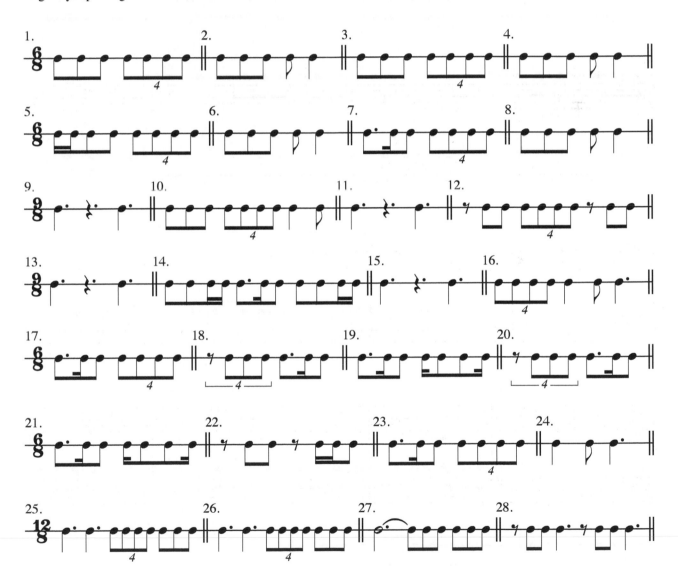

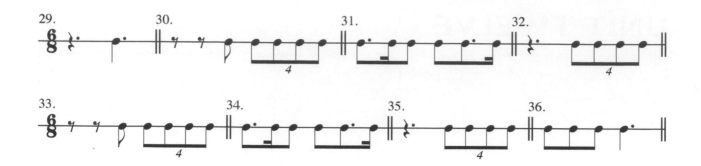

SECTION 2. Phrases

5. Rhythmic ostinato

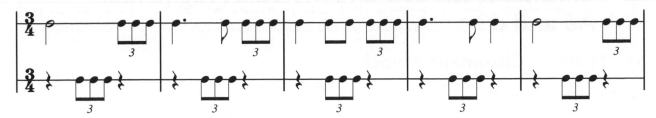

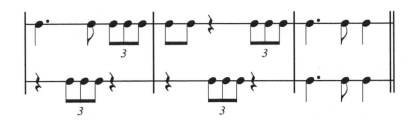

6. Rhythmic skeleton of Chopin (see 12E3, example 2)

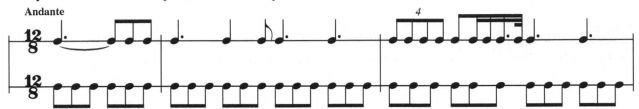

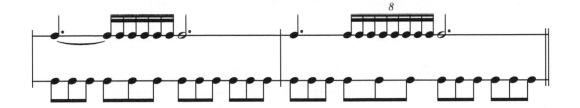

SECTION 3. Creating a Coherent Phrase

Using rhythmic patterns provided in section 1, create a coherent four-measure phrase.

Write your solution on the following line:

B Chromatic Models and Melodic Fragments: A6 and d3

SECTION 1. Chromatic Models

MODELS 1–2

The first model follows the contour of the A6 chord, outlining each factor. The second model demonstrates the resolution of the A6 to an octave on scale-degree 5.

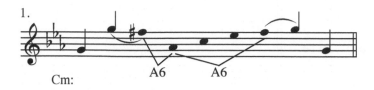

SECTION 2. Melodic Fragments in C Minor and C Major

Mozart *Die Zauberflöte* (The Magic Flute), no. 8, Finale (act 1) Tamino (transposed)

Mozart *La finta giardiniera* (Opera) (The Girl in Gardener's Disguise) (transposed)

3.

Mozart   Recitative from *Les noces de Figaro* (The Marriage of Figaro) (transposed)

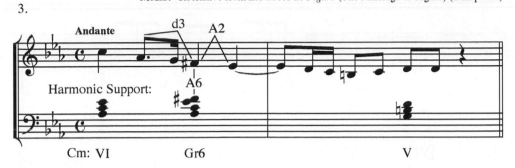

Cm: VI   Gr6   V

4.

Mozart   *La Clemenza di Tito* (Titus's Clemency) (transposed and abridged)

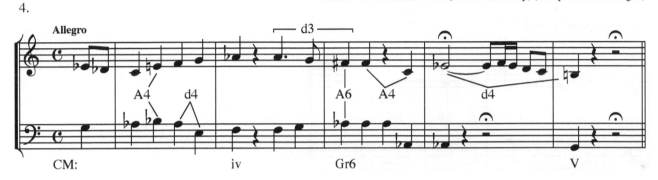

CM: iv   Gr6   V

5.

Mozart   *La Clemenza di Tito* (Titus's Clemency) (transposed and abridged)

CM: iv   I   iv   V   i   Fr6   V

6.

Mozart   *Les noces de Figaro* (The Marriage of Figaro) (transposed)

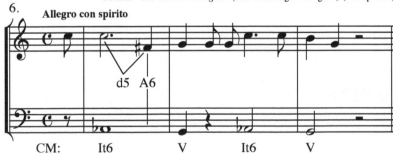

CM: It6   V   It6   V

Mozart *Les noces de Figaro* (The Marriage of Figaro) (transposed)

Allegro con spirito

CM: $[V^4_2]^*$ IV^6 $[V^4_2]$ IV^6 It6   V   It6   V

*Secondary dominant

7a. Reduction of no. 7.

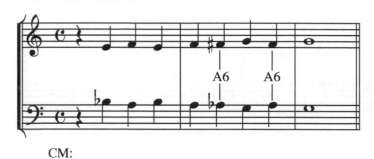

CM:

8.

Beethoven   Symphony no. 5, op. 67, II (transposed)

Andante con moto

Basic Harmony: Enharmonic

CM: I   V7 of IV   EM: Gr6*

Resolution

I$^6_4$ V^7 I

or V$^8_6_4$ ——— $^7_5_3$

* Functions as doubly A4

9.

Mozart *La finta giardiniera* (Opera) (The Girl in Gardener's Disguise) (transposed)

CM: I

D♯M: Gr6

I$^6_4$ V^7

or

V$^8_6_4$ ——— $^7_5_3$

10.

Mozart *Die Entführung aus dem Serail* (Opera) (The Abduction from the Seraglio) (transposed)

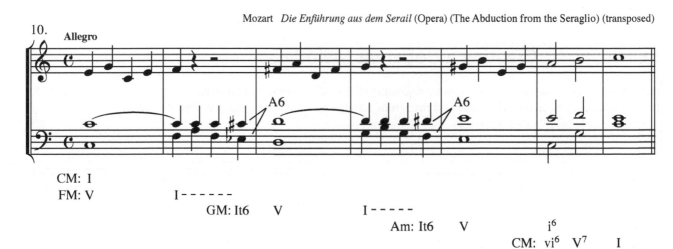

CM: I
FM: V   I - - - - - -
        GM: It6   V   I - - - - -
                    Am: It6   V   i^6
                            CM: vi^6 V^7 I

These supplemental fragments show voice-leading principles involving the diminished third (D♭–B♮) brought about by the motion of the lowered second scale degree (D♭) to the leading tone (B♮) and tonic (C).

Beethoven   Variations on "God Save the King," WoO 78 (Var. 5, m. 5)

11.

Cm: III$^6_4$ vii°7   i   N^6 [vii°7]   V   i

SECTION 3. Creating a Coherent Melody

Return to section 2 and select two or three segments of melodic fragments that would create a coherent melody. It may be necessary to change the meter and rhythm of certain segments, depending on your choice.

SECTION 4. Improvisation

Once again, we are returning to the vocalise pattern of Unit 7, B-4. By extending this pattern, it will be possible to reinterpret V^7 in the original key as a German augmented sixth chord in a new key that is a minor second lower than the original key. This extended vocalise pattern can be modified to give practice in using the Italian augmented sixth chord and the French augmented sixth chord in modulatory patterns.

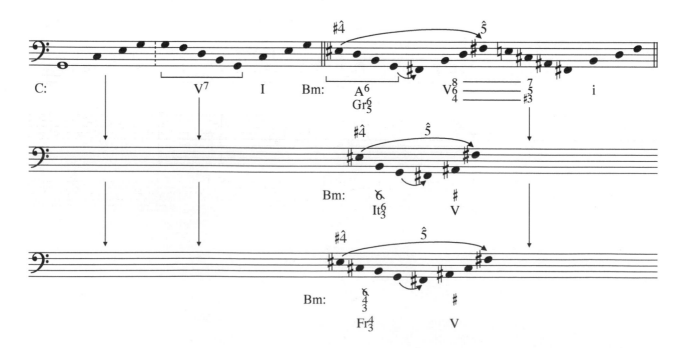

Use this fragment in C major from Bellini's *Come per me sereno* (How Peacefully for Me) from his opera *La Sonnambula* as an extended vocalise pattern to reinterpret the V⁷ as a German augmented sixth chord so that you can modulate to B minor. Improvise a new vocalise in B minor and move through the minor keys in descending motion: from B minor to B-flat minor and so on.

Bellini   *Come per me sereno* (How peacefully for me), from *La Sonnambula* (The Sleepwalker)

Adapted from *Come per me sereno* by Vincenzo Bellini, and published in *Embellished Opera Arias,* edited by Austin B. Caswell. Recent Researches in the Music of the Nineteenth and Early Twentieth Centuries, vols. 7–8. Madison, Wisconsin: A-R Editions, Inc. 1989. Used with permission.

Return to the improvisation patterns that you created in unit 7-B-4, based on fragments from Mozart's *The Magic Flute* and centered around the dominant 7th, and move through minor keys in descending motion.

C   Melodies with Modal Characteristics

Dies Irae (Day of Wrath) Gregorian chant (*Mass for the Dead*)

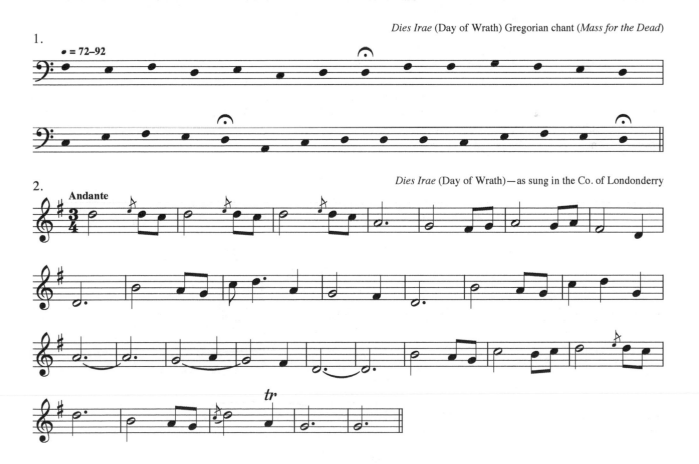

Dies Irae (Day of Wrath)—as sung in the Co. of Londonderry

3. "A Bold Child"   Ireland

Allegretto

Chorus

From *Songs of the Irish* by Donal O'Sullivan. Published by Mercier Press, Cork, Ireland. Used by permission.

4. "Barbara Ellen"

Allegro

BARBARA ELLEN from *80 Appalachian Folk Songs* collected by Cecil Sharp & Maude Karpeles. © Copyright 1968 by Faber Music, Ltd., London. Copyright Renewed. Reprinted by kind permission of Faber Music Ltd., London.

5. Hildegard von Bingen   *The Ursula Antiphons, 5. Deus Enim* (God Certainly) (transcribed and edited by Pozzi Escot)

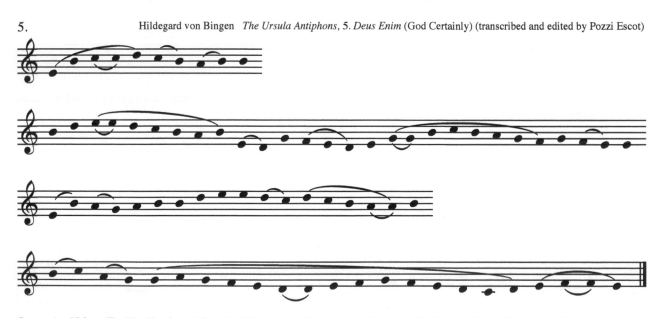

Deus enim, #5 from *The Nine Ursula Antiphons* by Hildegard von Bingen, transcribed and edited by Pozzi Escot. Reprinted with permission of Publication Contact International, Cambridge, MA.

6.   Hildegard von Bingen   *The Ursula Antiphons, 6. Aer Enim* (Air Certainly) (transcribed and edited by Pozzi Escot)

Aer enim, #8 from *The Nine Ursula Antiphons* by Hildegard von Bingen, transcribed and edited by Pozzi Escot. Reprinted with permission of Publication Contact International, Cambridge, MA.

"The Lone Rock" (Folk song)   Ireland

7.   **Andante**

From *Songs of the Irish* by Donal O'Sullivan. Published by Mercier Press, Cork, Ireland. Used by permission.

"Young Lad" (Folk song)   Ireland

8.   **Andantino**

From *Songs of the Irish* by Donal O'Sullivan. Published by Mercier Press, Cork, Ireland. Used by permission.

"My Sweetheart" Russian folk song

9.

Mussorgsky *Boris Godunov*, "Polonaise"

Alla polacca
10. **Non troppo allegro**

"The Fair Hills of E'ire O!" Irish folk song

11.
Poco sostenuto

From *Songs of the Irish* by Donal O'Sullivan. Published by Mercier Press, Cork, Ireland. Used by permission.

12. **Appassionato**

From *Songs of the Irish* by Donal O'Sullivan. Published by Mercier Press, Cork, Ireland. Used by permission.

Bulgarian folk song

13. **Allegro**

Charles Wakefield Cadman "He Who Moves in the Dew"*

14. **Allegretto con semplicità**

* A Chippewa Indian theme collected by Frances Densmore

15.

Cancionero Popular de la Provincia de Madrid Volume III, collected by Manuel Garcia Matos, critical edition by Juán Tomás Parés & José Romeu Figureas. Instituto Espanol de Musicología, Barcelona–Madrid 1960.

"The Blackthorn Tree"   Irish folk song

16. **Affettuoso**

From *Songs of the Irish* by Donal O'Sullivan. Published by Mercier Press, Cork, Ireland. Used by permission.

D Melodies

SECTION 1. Melodies by Schubert

Schubert *Wasserflut* (Flood of Tears), from *Winterreise* (Winter Journey), D. 911, no. 6

1. **Langsam**

Schubert *Rückblick* (Glance Back), from *Winterreise* (Winter Journey), D. 911, no. 8

2. **Nicht zu geschwind**

Schubert *Rast* (Rest), from *Winterreise* (Winter Journey), D. 911, no. 10

3. **Mässig**

Schubert *Im Dorfe* (In the Village), from *Winterreise* (Winter Journey), D. 911, no. 17

6. **Etwas langsam**

Schubert *Der Stürmische* (The Stormy Morning), from *Winterreise* (Winter Journey), D. 911, no. 18

7. **Ziemlich geschwind, doch dräftig**

Schubert *Täuschung* (Deception), from *Winterreise* (Winter Journey), D. 911, no. 19

8. **Etwas geschwind**

9.

Sehr langsam

10. **Ziemlich geschwind**

SECTION 2. Clef Reading and Transposition

Transpose this melody down a m3 by thinking in soprano clef. Substitute the A major key signature. The starting note is a (the a' above middle C).

Gustav Mahler *Das Trinklied vom Jammer der Erde* (The Drinking Song of the Earth's Lament),
from *Das Lied von der Erde* (The Song of the Earth)

1. **Allegro pesante with vigor**

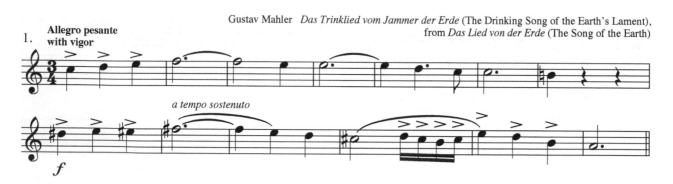

a tempo sostenuto

f

Transpose this melody down a m3 by thinking in soprano clef. Substitute the D major key signature for lines 1 and 2 and G major for lines 3 and 4. The starting note for each excerpt is:

Excerpt W: d" (octave and a 2nd above middle C)
Excerpt X: g' (above middle C)
Excerpt Y: c" (above middle C)

Gustav Mahler *Der Einsame im Herbst* (The Lonely One in Autumn), from *Das Lied von der Erde* (The Song of the Earth)

2. **Sostenuto**

Gustav Mahler *Von der Jugend* (Of Youth), from *Das Lied von der Erde* (The Song of the Earth)

3. **Behaglich heiter**

*1.2. Cl.
in B♭

* The clarinet is in B♭. Transpose down a M2 by thinking in tenor clef. Substitute the B♭ major key signature.
The starting note is b♭' (above middle C, c').

Transpose down a m3 by thinking in soprano clef. Substitute the key signature for G. The starting note is d.'

Gustav Mahler *Von der Jugend* (Of Youth), from *Das Lied von der Erde* (The Song of the Earth)

4. **Behaglich heiter**

Gustav Mahler *Nun will die Sonn' so hell aufgehn!* (Now the Sun Will Rise So Brightly),
from *Kinder-Totenlieder* (Songs on the Death of Children), no. 1

5. **Langsam und schwermitig, nicht schleppend**

9.

Andante

Reprinted by permission of G. Schirmer, Inc. (ASCAP).

E Ensembles and Play + Sing

SECTION 1. Repertoire Using Treble and Bass Clefs

Brahms *Ich weiss* (I Wonder Why the Dove So Sad Is Cooing!), from *Thirteen Canons*, op. 113, no. 11 (Text: Rückert)

1.

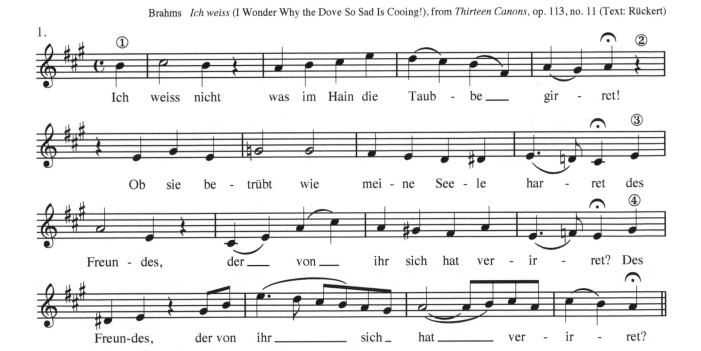

Ich weiss nicht was im Hain die Taub - be ___ gir - ret!

Ob sie be - trübt wie mei - ne See - le har - ret des

Freun - des, der ___ von ___ ihr sich hat ver - ir - ret? Des

Freun-des, der von ihr _____ sich ___ hat _____ ver - ir - ret?

Schubert *Liebe säuseln die Blätter* (The Leaves Rustle of Love), D988 (text from Hölty's *Maigesang*)

2.

Lie-be rie-selt die Quel - le, Lie-be flö - tet die Nach - ti-gall.

then, Lie-be rie - selt die Quel - le, Lie-be flö - tet die Nach-ti-gall.

Lie-be rie-selt die Quel - le, Lie-be flö - tet die Nach - ti-gall.

Lie-be säu-seln die Blät - ter, Lie-be duf-ten die Blü - then,

Lie-be säu-seln die Blät - ter, Lie-be duf-ten die Blü - then,

Lie - be säu - seln die Blät - ter, Lie - be duf - ten die Blü -

Lie-be rie-selt die Quel - le, Lie-be flö - tet die Nach - ti-gall.

Lie-be rie-selt die Quel - le, Lie-be flö - tet die Nach - ti-gall.

then, Lie-be rie - selt die Quel - le, Lie-be flö - tet die Nach-ti-gall.

Schütz *Introitus* (Introit), from *Die sieben Worte Jesu Christi* (The Seven Last Words of Christ)

SECTION 2. Repertoire Using C Clefs

Bach   Chorale *Ich hab' dich einen Augenblick* (I Have Forsaken You Only for a Moment, Dear Child) Cantata 103

Printed with the friendly permission of Breitkopf & Härtel, Wiesbaden.

SECTION 3. Play + Sing

1.

Chopin   Nocturne in E♭ major, op. 9, no. 2 (adapted and transposed)

2.

Chopin   Nocturne in E♭ major, op. 55, no. 2 (adapted)

UNIT THIRTEEN

A Rhythm—Further Subdivisions of the Beat: 4 against 3

SECTION 1. Models

Begin by chanting the numbers in time. Then chant the corresponding rhythmic pattern.

1.

(a) 1 2 3 4 5 6 7 8 9 10 11 12

(b) 1 . 3 . 5 . 7 . 9 . 11 .

(c) 1 . 3 4 . 6 7 . 9 10 . 12

(d) 1 2 . 4 5 . 7 8 . 10 11 .

(e) 1 . . 4 . . 7 . . 10 . .

(f) 1 . . 4 5 . 7 . 9 10 . .

2.

(a) 1 2 3 4 5 6 7 8 9 10 11 12

(b) 1 . 3 4 5 . 7 8 9 . 11 12

(c) 1 2 . 4 5 6 . 8 9 10 . 12

(d) 1 . . 4 5 . . 8 9 . . 12

(e) 1 . . . 5 . . . 9 . . .

(f) 1 . . 4 5 . 7 . 9 10 . .

3a.

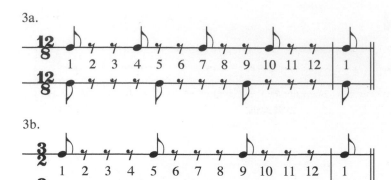

3b.

The authors thank Zachary Cairns for his help in developing the rhythmic materials in this section.

SECTION 2. Duets

1a.

1b.

2.

3.

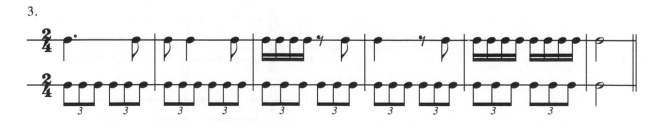

4.

5.

SECTION 3. Creating a Coherent Duet in 4 against 3

Using rhythmic patterns provided in section 2, create a coherent four-measure phrase.

Write your solution on the following lines:

B Diatonic and Chromatic Models and Melodic Fragments: d4

SECTION 1. Diatonic and Chromatic Models

The models in this section emphasize the diminished 4th (d4) and relate to the music of Ellington, Liszt, Bach, Beethoven, Haydn, and Schubert (see section 2). The models (exercises) of this section prefigure the fragments in the following manner:

Models	Fragments
1, 2	1, 2
3, 4	3, 4
5	5, 6, 7
6	5, 8
7	10
8	8, 10

For further practice, sing exercise 5 in all minor keys, transposing to each new key by P5 down or P4 up (see model below).

SECTION 2. Melodic Fragments in A♭ Major and F Minor

A♭ major:

1.

Ellington "Mood Indigo"

MOOD INDIGO from SOPHISTICATED LADIES. Words and music by Duke Ellington, Irving Mills, and Albany Bigard. Copyright © 1931 (Renewed 1958) and Assigned to EMI Mills Music, Inc., Famous Music Corporation, and Indigo Mood Music c/o The Songwriters Guild of America in the U.S.A. Rights for the world outside the U.S.A. controlled by EMI Mills Music, Inc. (Publishing) and Alfred Publishing Co., Inc. (Print). International copyright secured. All rights reserved.

2.

Haydn String Quartet op. 76, no. 4, I (transposed) (adapted)

3.

Haydn *Das strickende Mädchen* (The Knitting Girl) (transposed)

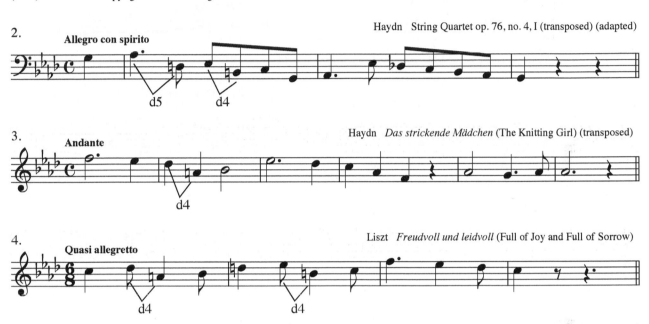

4.

Liszt *Freudvoll und leidvoll* (Full of Joy and Full of Sorrow)

F Minor:

5.

Schubert *Der Doppelgänger* (The Wraith) (transposed)

6.

Bach Fugue no. 4 from *Well-Tempered Clavier*, Book I (transposed)

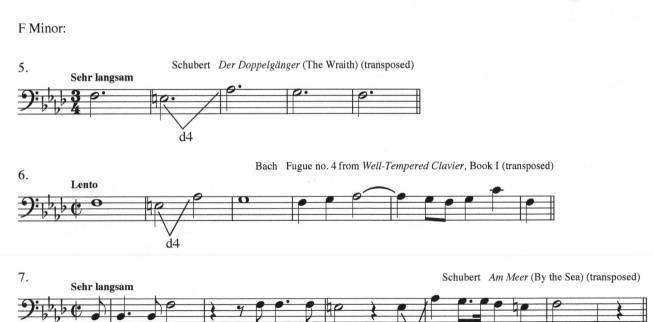

7.

Schubert *Am Meer* (By the Sea) (transposed)

SECTION 3. Creating a Coherent Melody

Return to section 2 and select two or three segments of melodic fragments that create a coherent melody. It may be necessary to change the meter and rhythm of certain segments, depending on your choice.

SECTION 4. Improvisation

Use the first four measures of Duke Ellington's "Mood Indigo" (see melodic fragment 1) as the basis for an improvisation. In case you are wondering how the rest of the tune goes, look at melody 3 in section D of this unit. Use your improvisation as a backdrop for your own words or for the original text which is as follows:

*Mood Indigo**

You ain't been blue; no, no, no.
You ain't been blue,
Till you've had that mood indigo.
That feelin' goes stealin' down to my shoes
While I sit and sigh, "Go 'long blues."

Always get that mood indigo.
Since my baby said goodbye.
In the evenin' when lights are low,
I'm so lonesome I could cry.

'Cause there's nobody who cares about me,
I'm just a soul who's bluer than blue can be.
When I get that mood indigo,
I could lay me down and die.

C Melodies Related to Jazz

SECTION 1. The Blues Repertoire

These melodies are by composers such as Chris Smith, Perry Bradford, and Cab Calloway.

Chris Smith "Ballin' the Jack"

1. Moderato

2.

Moderato Chris Smith "Boom, Tum, Ta-Ra-Ra—Zing Boom!" Lyrics by Ferd. E. Mierisch

Boom, tum-ta - ra - ra   Zing Boom!

Boom, tum-ta - ra - ra   Zing Boom!

Boom, Tum, Ta-Ra - Ra -   Zing Boom!

Boom tum-ta - ra - ra! Zing   Boom! Zing

3.

Perry Bradford "That Thing Called Love"

Moderato

4.   Perry Bradford "Crazy Blues"

SECTION 2. Vocalise by Alec Wilder

This vocalise was written for Eileen Farrell by Alec Wilder in 1972. It represents an interesting blend of classical and jazz idioms.

Wilder *Vocalise* 1

D   Melodies by Duke Ellington

Chord changes for the Ellington melodies are given to inspire your keyboard harmonizations. Whenever possible, harmonize the melodies and accompany them as you sing.

Billy Strayhorn and the Delta Rhythm Boys   "Take the 'A' Train"

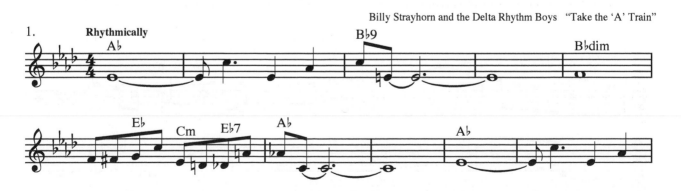

Duke Ellington, Eddie DeLange, and Irving Mills   "Solitude"

2. **Slowly, with expression**

Duke Ellington, Irving Mills, and Albany Bigard   "Mood Indigo"

3. **Slowly**

Duke Ellington, Irving Mills, and Manny Kurtz   "In a Sentimental Mood"

4. **Slowly with expression**

Duke Ellington and Billy Strayhorn   "Day Dream"

5. **Slow**

Duke Ellington, Irving Mills, Henry Nemo, and John Redmond   "I Let a Song Go Out of My Heart"

6. **Slowly**

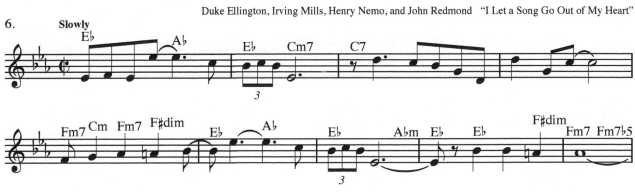

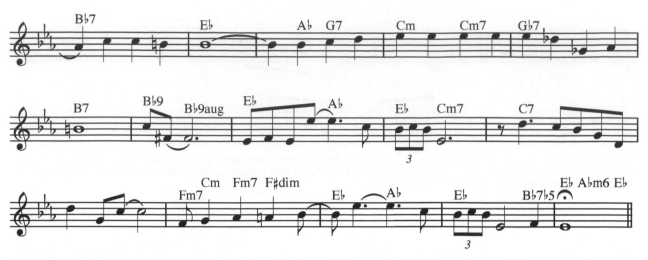

E Ensembles and Play + Sing

SECTION 1. Repertoire Using Treble and Bass Clefs

James Weldon Johnson and R. Rosamond Johnson   "Lift Every Voice and Sing" (National Negro Hymn)

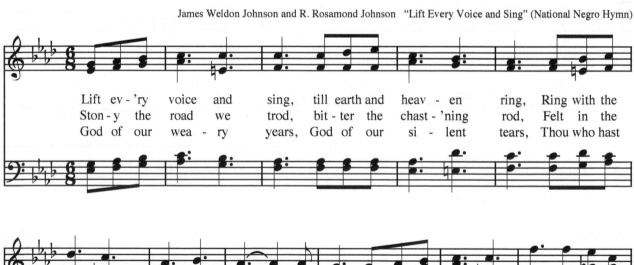

Lift ev - 'ry   voice   and   sing,   till earth and   heav - en   ring,   Ring with the
Ston - y   the   road   we   trod,   bit - ter   the   chast - 'ning   rod,   Felt in the
God of our   wea - ry   years, God of our   si - lent   tears,   Thou who hast

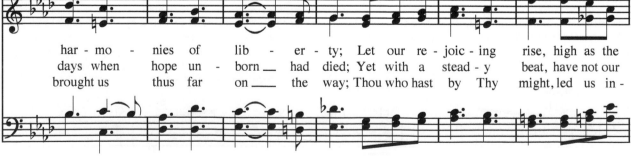

har - mo - nies   of   lib - er - ty;   Let our re - joic - ing   rise, high as the
days when   hope un - born__ had   died; Yet with a   stead - y   beat, have not our
brought us   thus far   on ___   the   way; Thou who hast by Thy   might, led us in -

lis - t'ning ___ skies, Let it re - sound loud as the roll - ing sea. ___
wea - ry ___ feet Come to the place for which our fa - thers sighed? ___
to the ___ light, Keep us for - ev - er in the path, ___ we pray. ___

Sing a song full of the faith that the dark past has taught us,
We have come o - ver a way that with tears has been wa - tered,
Lest our feet stray from the pla - ces, our God, where we met Thee,

Sing a song full of the hope that the pres - ent has brought ___
We have come, tread - ing our path thro' the blood of the slaugh -
Lest our hearts, drunk with the wine of the world, we for - get ___

ff

us; Fac - ing the ris - ing sun of our new day be -
tered, Out from the gloom - y past, till now we stand at ___
Thee; Sha - dowed be - neath Thy hand, may we for - ev - er ___

gun,   Let   us   march   on   till   vic - to - ry _____   is   won.
last   Where the white gleam of   our bright star _____   is   cast.
stand, True to   our   God,   true to   our   na - tive land.

SECTION 2. Repertoire Using C Clefs

Just as in unit 11 E-2 where we had a puzzle canon from Bach's Musical Offering with Kirnberger's solution, here we have another intriguing example from the same work. In this case, the original melody (left to right) is designed to appear in retrograde (right to left) in the second part. This process is known as *cancrizans*.

1.   Bach *Musikalisches Opfer* (The Musical Offering), BWV 1079

2. Bach   Kirnberger

Here is a puzzle canon by Schoenberg, written in 1934. Notice how Schoenberg follows the same compositional technique as Bach in using the original theme in retrograde.

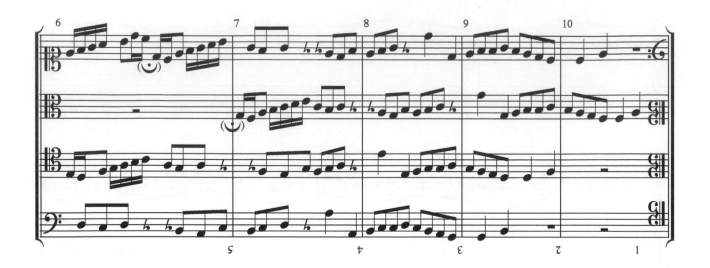

SECTION 3. Play + Sing

1.

Chopin Nocturne in D major, op. 9, no. 3 (transposed and adapted)

Allegretto ♩. = 66

p

A simpler version of the piano's left hand part for mm. 5–11 would be: Repeat the pitch found on each downbeat for the entire bar, but use the same rhythmic values as the original throughout.

2.

A simpler version of the piano's left hand part for mm. 5–8 would be: Repeat the pitch found on each downbeat for two beats, then repeat the pitch found on each third beat for two beats; use the same rhythmic values as the original throughout.

Debussy Prélude, *Pour le Piano* (adapted)

3.

UNIT FOURTEEN

A   Rhythm—Irregular or Additive Meter

SECTION 1.   Phrases in Irregular or Additive Meter

1.

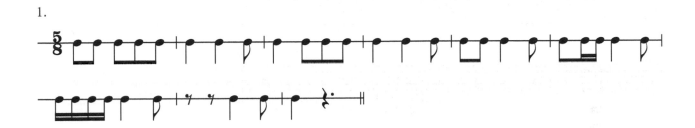

2.

(based on unit 14–D–2, example 4   Tchaikovsky, Symphony #6: II)

3.

4.

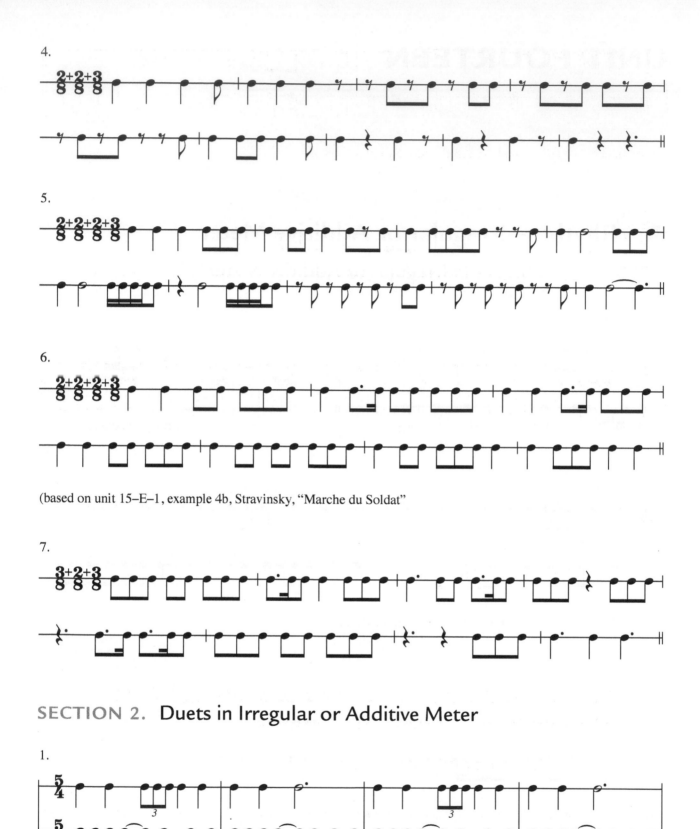

5.

6.

(based on unit 15–E–1, example 4b, Stravinsky, "Marche du Soldat"

7.

SECTION 2. Duets in Irregular or Additive Meter

1.

(based on unit 14–D–2, example 4, Tchaikovsky, Symphony #6: II)

2.

SECTION 3. Creating a Coherent Phrase in Irregular or Additive Meter

Using rhythmic patterns provided in section 1, create a coherent four-measure phrase.

Write your solution on the following line:

B Modal Mixture and Enharmonic Modulation Models and Melodic Fragments

SECTION 1. Diatonic and Chromatic Models

The models in this section emphasize modal mixture, enharmonic changes, motivic structure, chromatic, whole-tone, and octatonic fragments. The musical fragments (section 2) that correspond with each of the models in this section are as follows:

Models	Elements of Mixture		Fragments
1, 2	F♭		1
3, 4	F♭	D, C♭	2
5		C♭, B♭♭	3
6	F♭, E♭♭, D, C♭, B♭♭		4

MODELS 1–6

a. Mixture

The first four models contain elements of modal mixture. For practice, sing example 1a, with one of your colleagues singing 1b, and so on.

b. Enharmonic changes (chromatic modulation)

Models	Enharmonic Changes	Fragments
7a, a', a''	A♭ = G♯	5
	G♭ = F♯	
	D♭ = C♯	
7b, 7b'		6

MODEL 7

The motives of examples 7a, 7a', and 7a'' represent different orderings of the same intervallic patterns: M2, m3 (or M6), and P4. Examples 7b and 7b' represent the pattern m2 and M3 (outlining a P4).

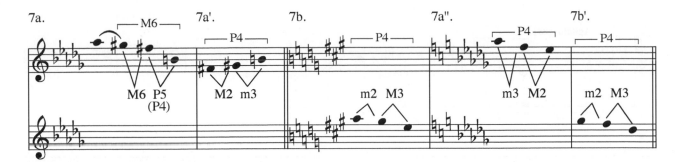

7a.   7a'.   7b.   7a".   7b'.

c. Motivic structure

Models	Fragments
8a	7a, 7b
8b	8a, 8b

MODEL 8

8a.   8b.

SECTION 2. Melodic Fragments: All Intervals

Sing the following melodic fragments until you can sing them without error.

a. Mixture

1.

Del Tredici   *The Acrostic Song* (Alice Pleasance Liddell) from *Final Alice* (transposed)

Andante sostenuto

Meas.   7   8   9   10   11   12

Meas.   21   22   23   24   25   26

ACROSTIC SONG from FINAL ALICE (Del Tredici) © Copyright 1978 by Boosey & Hawkes, Inc. Reprinted by permission.

2.

Liszt   *Der Hirt* (The Shepherd) (transposed) (abridged)

Andante pastorale

Meas.   20   21   22   23

Meas.   83   84   88   89

3. Liszt *Pace non trovo* (I Find No Peace) (Petrarch Sonnet) (transposed)

4. Prokofiev *Sladkaya pesenka* (Sweet Melody), op. 68, no. 2

Sweet Melody from *Three Children's Songs for Piano,* Op. 68 by Sergei Prokofiev. Copyright © 1946 (Renewed) by G. Schirmer, Inc. (ASCAP) International Copyright Secured. All Rights Reserved. Reprinted by permission.

b. Modulation—enharmonic changes

5. Liszt *Der Fischerknabe* (The Fisher Lad)

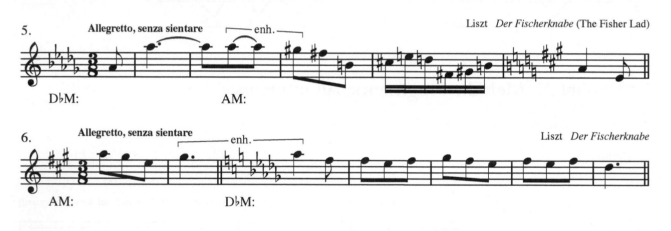

6. Liszt *Der Fischerknabe*

c. Motivic structure

7a. Brahms Symphony no. 3, II (transposed)

7b. Brahms Ballade op. 118, no. 3 (transposed)

8a.

Langsam und leise

Brahms   *Immer leiser wird mein Schlummer* (Fretful Slumber), op. 105, no. 2 (transposed)

8b.

Andante

Brahms   Piano Concerto no. 2, op. 83, III (transposed)

SECTION 3. Creating a Coherent Melody

Return to section 2 and select two or three segments of melodic fragments that create a coherent melody. It may be necessary to change the meter and rhythm of certain segments, depending on your choice.

SECTION 4. Improvisation

1. Return to the "vocalise pattern" that was introduced in unit 7-B, section 4, and expand this pattern to incorporate elements of "mixture" through improvisation.

Vocalise pattern

Example of an improvised vocalise pattern with mixture

Choose one of the melodic fragments that illustrates "mixture" (1–4) as the basis for an improvisation.

2. Return to the "vocalise pattern" that was introduced in unit 7-B, section 4, and expand this pattern to incorporate an "enharmonic change" that results in a "chromatic modulation" through improvisation.

Vocalise pattern

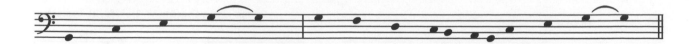

Example of an improvised vocalise pattern with an enharmonic change (chromatic modulation)

Choose one of the melodic fragments that illustrates enharmonic change (chromatic modulation) (5–6) as the basis for an improvisation.

3. Return to the "vocalise pattern" that was introduced in Unit 7-B, section 4, and expand this pattern to incorporate a "motivic structure" that develops through improvisation.

Vocalise pattern

Example of an improvised vocalise pattern with a motivic structure that develops

Choose one of the melodic fragments that illustrates a motivic structure that develops (7–8) as the basis for an improvisation.

4. Return to the "vocalise pattern" that was introduced in unit 7-B, section 4, and expand this pattern to incorporate chromatic, whole-tone, or octatonic elements through improvisation.

Vocalise pattern

Example of an improvised vocalise pattern that incorporates chromatic, whole-tone, or octatonic elements through improvisation

Choose one of the melodic fragments (9–10) that illustrates chromatic, whole-tone, or octatonic elements as the basis for an improvisation.

C Twentieth-Century Cabaret Song by Arnold Schoenberg

Schoenberg *Jedem das Seine* (To Each His Own) (text by Colly) June, 1901

Used by permission of Belmont Music Publishers, Pacific Palisades, CA 90272

D Twentieth-Century Songs

SECTION 1. Art Songs by Ravel and Holst

Ravel *Soupir* (Sigh), from *Trois Poèmes de Stéphane Mallarmé* (Three Poems of Stéphane Mallarmé), I (dedicated to Igor Stravinsky)

1.

Soupir (Sigh), from *Trois Poèmes de Stéphane Mallarmé* (Three Poems of Stéphane Mallarmé), I (dedicated to Igor Stravinsky), *Maurice Ravel Songs 1896–1914,* edited by Arbie Orenstein. Copyright 1990 by Dover Publications, Inc. All rights reserved under Pan American and International Copyright Conventions.

Ravel *Kaddisch* (Kaddish), from *Deux Mélodies Hébraïques* (Two Hebrew Melodies)

2.

Kaddisch (Kaddish), from *Deux Mélodies Hébraïques* (Two Hebrew Melodies), *Maurice Ravel Songs 1896–1914,* edited by Arbie Orenstein.
Copyright 1990 by Dover Publications, Inc. All rights reserved under Pan American and International Copyright Conventions.

L'Enigme Eternelle (The Eternal Enigma), from *Deux Mélodies Hébraïques* (Two Hebrew Melodies), *Maurice Ravel Songs 1896–1914,* edited by Arbie Orenstein. Copyright 1990 by Dover Publications, Inc. All rights reserved under Pan American and International Copyright Conventions.

4.   Holst   *Persephone*

Persephone, from *Twelve Humbert Wolfe Songs* by Gustav Holst. © 1930 by Augener, Ltd. Published by Galliard Ltd.

SECTION 2. Melodies by Stravinsky, Rossini, Tchaikovsky, and Folk Song

Rossini *Du séjour de la lumière* (From the Abode of Life), from *La siège de Corinthe* (The Siege of Corinth)

Adapted from *Du séjour de la lumière* (From the Abode of Life) by Gioacchino Rossini and published in *Embellished Opera Arias,* edited by Austin B. Caswell. Recent Researches in the Music of the Nineteenth and Early Twentieth Centuries, vols. 7–8. Madison, Wisconsin: A-R Editions, Inc., 1989. Used with permission.

4.
Allegro con grazia (♩ = 144)   Tchaikovsky   Symphony no. 6 (op. 74): II

E Ensembles and Play + Sing

SECTION 1. Repertoire Using Treble and Bass Clefs

Stravinsky   *Perséphone*

C.a

En - core ___ mal ré - veil - lé - e   Per - sé - pho - ne é - mer - veil - lé - e

T.

Per - sé - pho - ne é - mer - veil - lé - e

SECTION 2. Repertoire Using C Clefs

Schoenberg *Für Alban Berg zum 9. Februar 1935* written in honor of Alban Berg's 50th birthday

Freu - de her - ein!   Wie kannst du fra - gen?   Darf ich

Ehr',   bringst Freu - de her - ein!   Wie kannst du fra - gen?

ein!   Wie kannst du fra - gen?   Darf ich ein - tre - ten . . ?

de her - ein! ____   Wie kannst du fra - gen?   Darf ich ein -

Used by permission of Belmont Music Publishers, Pacific Palisades, CA 90272

SECTION 3. Play + Sing

Holst *The Planets*, "Mars" (adapted)

1.

2.

UNIT FIFTEEN

A   Rhythm—Changing Meter with Constant Pulse

SECTION 1. Phrases in Changing Meter

1.

See unit 15–C, example 12, Bernstein, Symphony #1: III "Lamentation"

4.

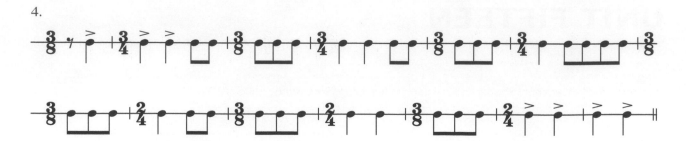

See unit 15–E–1, example 4b, Stravinsky, "Marche du Soldat," *Histoire du Soldat* (adapted)

5.

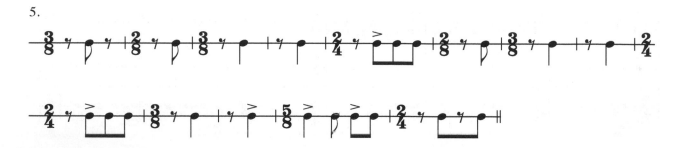

See unit 15–E–1, example 5b, Stravinsky, "Danse Sacrale," *Le Sacre du Printemps* (adapted)

6.

See unit 15–E–1, example 6b, Stravinsky, Symphonies of Wind Instruments: I

7.

See unit 15–E–1, example 7b, Stravinsky, "Bransle Gay," *Agon* (adapted)

8

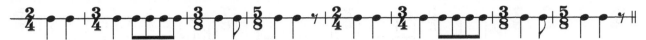

See unit 15–E–1, example 8b, Bartok, "Change of Time," *Mikrokosmos*, Vol. 5, #126

SECTION 2. Ensembles in Changing Meters

1.

See unit 15–E–1, example 4b, Stravinsky, "Marche du Soldat," *Histoire du Soldat* (adapted)

2.

See unit 15–E–1, example 7b, Stravinsky, "Bransle Gay," *Agon* (adapted)

SECTION 3. Creating a Coherent Phrase in Changing Meter

Using rhythmic patterns provided in section 1, create a coherent four-measure phrase.

Write your solution on the following line:

B Whole-tone, Octatonic, and Atonal Models and Melodic Fragments: All Intervals

SECTION 1. Atonal Models

I. The exercises in this section are atonal.

Within the atonal context, a few whole-tone and octatonic patterns are found. All exercises relate to the music of Strauss, Schoenberg, Debussy, and Bartók.

Each model in this section is related to the same corresponding number in the fragments. Each exercise has several segments (example 1: segments a–d) to encourage class participation by as many individuals as possible. One sings *a* while the next repeats *a* and continues with *b* and so on. For these atonal exercises, you should use whatever solfeggio or number system your instructor suggests.

MODELS 1–2

Model 1 focuses on the M6 and m2.

Model 2 is a study in 7ths.

MODELS 3 AND 4

Model 3 is based on a six-note pattern (later known as pitch-class set 6–Z4).

Sing the outer voices; the inner voices are provided to establish context.

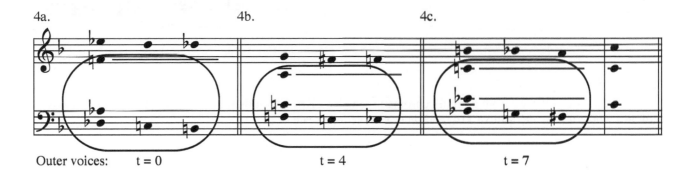

Outer voices: t = 0   t = 4   t = 7

MODELS 5–10

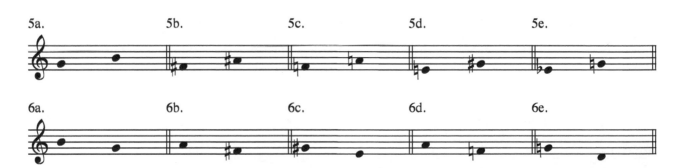

Models 7–10 should be sung in ensemble.

MODEL 11

These models are extracted from a highly chromatic song by Liszt. Altogether, these three motives (11a, b, and c) outline a whole-tone scale. Motive 11d represents a whole-tone scale.

MODEL 12

These models are extracted from Schoenberg's *Gurrelieder* (Songs of Guerre). Each pattern constitutes an *octatonic pentad*.

SECTION 2. Melodic Fragments: All Intervals

R. Strauss *Salome*, op. 54

1.

Schoenberg *Pelléas et Mélisande*, op. 5

2.

Used by permission of Belmont Music Publishers, Pacific Palisades, CA 90272.

Schoenberg *Pelléas et Mélisande*, op. 5

3.

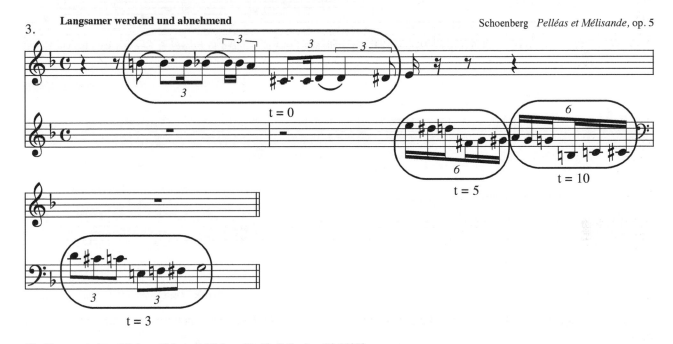

Used by permission of Belmont Music Publishers, Pacific Palisades, CA 90272.

4. Molto allegro

Strauss *Salome*

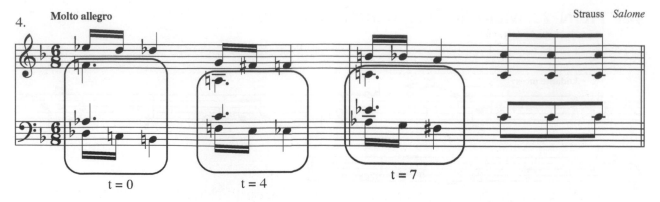

t = 0   t = 4   t = 7

5.

Debussy *Pelléas et Mélisande* (Opera)

De plus en plus animé

6. ♪ = 116

Bartók *A kékszakállú herceg vára* (The Castle of Duke Bluebeard) (Opera), op. 11

© Copyright 1921 by Universal Edition; Copyright Renewed. Copyright and Renewal assigned to Boosey & Hawkes, Inc., for the U.S.A. Reprinted by permission.

7. Più mosso

Strauss *Salome*

8. In gehender Bewegung

Schoenberg *Pelléas et Mélisande*, op. 5

Used by permission of Belmont Music Publishers, Pacific Palisades, CA 90272.

9. Meno mosso

Bartók *The Castle of Duke Bluebeard*, op. 11

© 1921 by Universal Edition; Copyright Renewed. Copyright and Renewal assigned to Boosey & Hawkes, Inc., for the U.S.A. Reprinted by permission.

10. Un peu animé

Debussy *Pelléas et Mélisande*

t = 0   t = 2   Whole Tone

11.

Liszt "Mignons Lied" (Mignon's Song)

Molto lento e con ardore

Schoenberg *Gurrelieder* (Songs of Gurre), "Die wilde Jagd" (The Wild Chase) (octave lower).
Students are encouraged to alternate in the singing of motives a and b.

12.

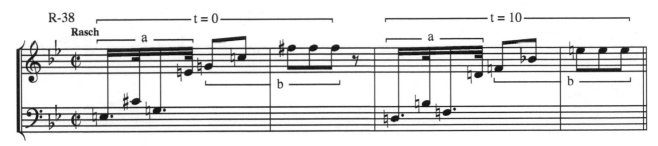

SECTION 3. Creating a Coherent Melody

Return to section 2 and select two or three segments of melodic fragments that create a coherent melody. It may be necessary to change the meter and rhythm of certain segments, depending on your choice.

SECTION 4. Improvisation

Return to unit 14, part D, section 2 and review the vocalises by Stravinsky (*Pastorale*) and Rossini (*Du séjour de la lumière* [From the Abode of Life]). Notice that both of these examples are in major keys and emphasize raised scale degree 4 and lowered scale degree 7.

The two rhythmic reductions that follow are derived from the Stravinsky *Pastorale* (1) and the Rossini (*Du séjour de la lumière* [From the Abode of Life]) (2). Use these reductions as models for improvisations.

C Twentieth-Century Melodies

This section contains works by Milhaud, Debussy, Menotti, Griffes, Bernstein, Weill, Trinkley, Barsom, and others.

Milhaud   *La Création du Monde* (The Creation of the World)

Milhaud   *La Création du Monde* (The Creation of the World)

3.

Santa Rosalia. Copyright © 1994 Bruce Trinkley and J. Jason Charnesky.

Paul Barsom "On Imminent Rays"

4.

"On Imminent Rays" by Paul Barsom. Copyright © 1989 Ringing Change Music. Reprinted by permission of Paul Barsom, State College, PA.

Debussy String Quartet op. 10, III

5.

Debussy *Des pas sur la neige* (Footsteps in the Snow), Book I, Prelude VI

6.

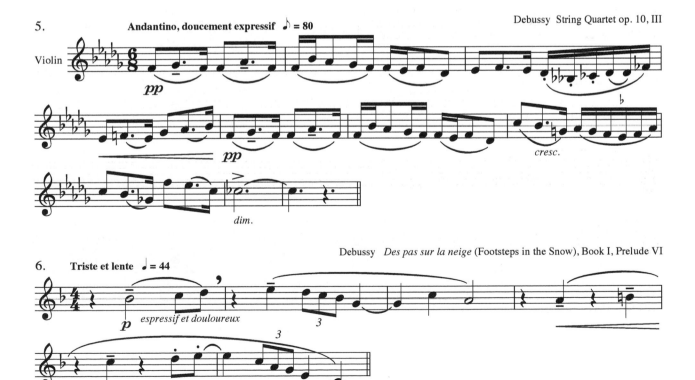

Debussy *La fille aux cheveux de lin* (The Girl with the Flaxen Hair), Book I, Prelude VIII

7.

Tré calme et doucement expressif ♩ = 60

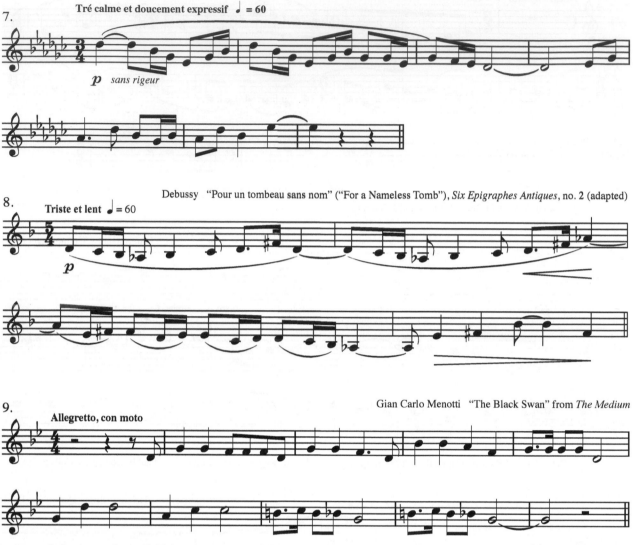

8.

Debussy "Pour un tombeau sans nom" ("For a Nameless Tomb"), *Six Epigraphes Antiques*, no. 2 (adapted)

Triste et lent ♩ = 60

9.

Gian Carlo Menotti "The Black Swan" from *The Medium*

Allegretto, con moto

10.

Languidamente (♩ = 72–80)

Charles T. Griffes *Symphony in Yellow*, op. 3, no. 2

SYMPHONY IN YELLOW OP. 3 NO. 2. By Charles T. Griffes. © 1943 (Renewed) by G. Schirmer, Inc. (ASCAP) International Copyright Secured. All Rights Reserved. Reprinted by Permission.

Leonard Bernstein   "It Must Be Me" (reprise of "It Must Be So") from *Candide*

11.   **Very slowly and freely, like a folk song**

IT MUST BE SO from CANDIDE (Bernstein) © Copyright 1955, 1957, 1974, 1982, 1990 by Amberson Holdings, LLC. Copyright Renewed. Publisher Boosey & Hawkes, Inc., Sole Agent. Reprinted by permission.

12. Lento

13.

Kurt Weill "The Lonesome Dove" from *Down in the Valley*

Moderato assai

THE LONESOME DOVE from DOWN IN THE VALLEY By Kurt Weill. Copyright © 1948 (Renewed) by G. Schirmer, Inc. (ASCAP). International Copyright Secured. All Rights Reserved. Reprinted by Permission.

14.

Kodaly *Valsette*

Allegro (♩. = 80)

© Copyright 1910 by Rozsavolgyi and Co. Budapest; Copyright assigned to Editio Musica Budapest for the World. Reprinted by permission of Boosey & Hawkes, Inc., Sole Agent.

Presto ♩ = 108
(to be transposed down an 8ve)

15.

Bartók   Bagatelle no. 14 from *Fourteen Bagatelles*, op. 6

Munter. Schnelle Viertel
(to be transposed down an 8ve)

16.

Hindemith   *Kleine Klaviermusik* (Short Piano Music), no. 3

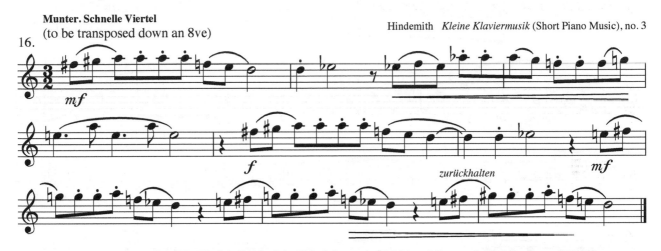

Stravinsky   *Berceuse*

17.   ♩ = 88

D Vocalises by Honegger and Martinů

1.

Honegger *Vocalise-étude*

Reproduced with amiable authorization from Editions Alphonse Leduc-Paris.

2.

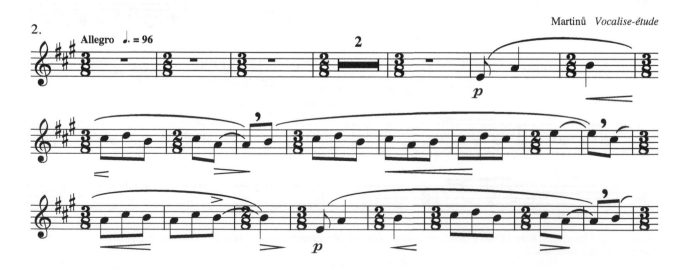

Martinů *Vocalise-étude*

Reproduced with amiable authorization from Editions Alphonse Leduc-Paris.

E Ensembles of the Twentieth Century

SECTION 1. Repertoire Using Treble and Bass Clefs

The following ensemble excerpts should be performed vocally, although instruments may be used to supplement voices. In addition to singing or playing parts in ensemble, you are encouraged to play entire excerpts at the keyboard.

PROCEDURE

1. Students should sing the melodic "reduction" of each excerpt, using whatever system is suggested by the instructor—solfege, numbers (1–8 or 0–11).
2. Students should take turns singing or playing individual lines of these excerpts before singing or playing them in ensemble.
3. Whenever possible, the instructor should bring recordings to class so that students will come to a full understanding of the musical context for each excerpt.

Example 1 (Milhaud) can be related to the melodic pattern, which encompasses six notes of the major scale:

1. From mi up to do (mi, fa, sol, la, ti, do), or
2. From 3 up to 1 (3, 4, 5, 6, 7, 1), or
3. From 4 up to 0 (4, 5, 7, 9, 11, 0)

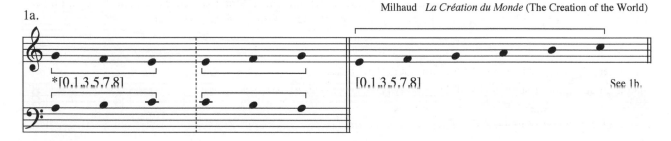

Milhaud *La Création du Monde* (The Creation of the World)

1a.

*[0,1,3,5,7,8]   [0,1,3,5,7,8]   See 1b.

Milhaud, *La Création du Monde* (The Creation of the World), (1923).

*For further explanation, see Allen Forte, *The Structure of Atonal Music*. New Haven, CT, Yale University Press, 1973.

Example 2 (Debussy) introduces a recurring four-note pattern (tetrachord) in the second violin part, which encompasses four notes of the major scale:

1. From ti up to fa (ti, do, re, [mi], fa), or
2. From 7 up to 4 (7, 1, 2, [3], 4), or
3. From 11 up to 5 (11, 0, 2, [4], 5)

In the same example, the viola part has a recurring six-note pattern (hexachord), which can be thought of *at first* in two different tonalities:

1. First three notes: do, ti, sol; last three notes: re, fa, sol
2. First three notes: 1, 7, 5; last three notes: 2, 4, 5

Ultimately, students should be encouraged to think in terms of all twelve notes, with C being zero:

3. 7, 6, 2, 5, 8, 10

Whenever this six-note pattern is placed in "normal order" (see Forte's *Structure of Atonal Music*), the "pitch-class set" corresponds to 6-Z39 in Forte's taxonomy.

2, 5, 6, 7, 8, 10 and reduced to "zero level" (Forte)
0, 3, 4, 5, 6, 8 and inverted
0, 2, 3, 4, 5, 8

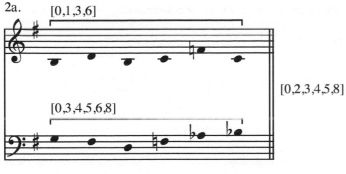

Debussy String Quartet op. 10, II (m. 10)

2a.

[0,1,3,6]

[0,2,3,4,5,8]

[0,3,4,5,6,8]

See 3b.

Example 3 (Debussy) features a three-note pattern in various transformations (cello). Although it is possible to think of each three-note pattern in its own tonality (la, do, si; do, si, ti), it is more beneficial for the student to recognize the pattern of alternating M3s and m3s, or alternating "interval classes" (Forte), which form [0,1,4]:

ic 3 (interval class three), encompassing three half-steps = m3
ic 4 (interval class four), encompassing four half-steps = M3
In combination, the first six notes of the cello part are entirely chromatic.

In the same part (cello) at the end of the first measure, the last five notes are a d7 chord: 0,3,6,9. Both of these melodic ideas are prominent in measure 19:

Melodically, [0,1,4] is found in all four parts.
Harmonically, [0,3,6,9] is found when all four parts are combined.

Debussy String Quartet op. 10, IV (m. 15)

3a.   meas. 19

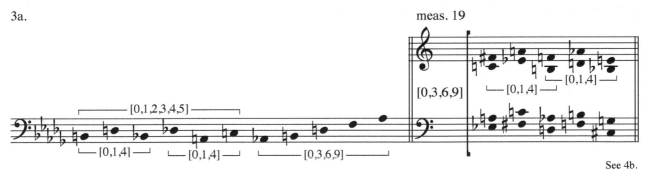

See 4b.

2b.

3b.

Stravinsky "Marche du Soldat," *Histoire du Soldat* (adapted)

Stravinsky "Danse Sacrale," *Le Sacre du Printemps*

5b.

6b.

Stravinsky "Bransle Gay," *Agon* (adapted)

7b.

Bartók "Change of Time," *Mikrokosmos*, Vol. 5, #126 (adapted)

8b.

SECTION 2. Repertoire Using C Clefs

Schoenberg   Canon in 3 keys for the Genossenschaft Deutscher Tonsetzer

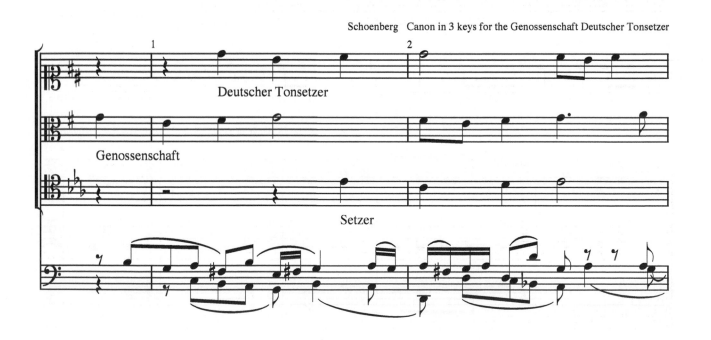

Deutscher Tonsetzer

Genossenschaft

Setzer

Canon in Three Keys for the Genossenschaft Deutscher Tonsetze. Copyright © 1963 Bärenreiter-Verlag, Kassel. Reprinted by permission.

1.

Bartók "Song of the Harvest" Forty-Four Violin Duos, #33

2. Allegro ♩ = 136–144

Durufle *Requiem, Introit*

3. Andante moderato (♩ = 60)

UNIT SIXTEEN

A   Rhythm—Polymeter

SECTION 1. Ensembles in Polymeter

1.

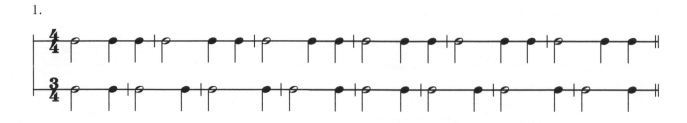

2.

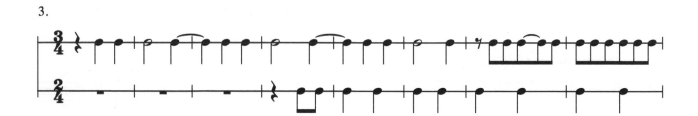

3.

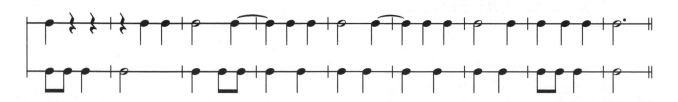

See unit 16–E–3, example 2, Stravinsky, *Petrushka*, Tableau III (adapted)

4.

See unit 15–E–1, Stravinsky, "Marche du Soldat" (adapted)

5.

See unit 16–E–3, Holst, St. Paul's Suite

B Twelve-Tone Models and Melodic Fragments for Interval Study

SECTION 1. Models: Dyads, Trichords, Tetrachords, Pentachords, and Hexachords

All exercises in this section are of the 12-tone type and relate to the first example (only) in section 2. The format for building exercises for interval study is illustrated for the first exercise. By using this approach, all 20 of the excerpts in section 2 will be made much easier to accomplish.

To provide as much individual participation as possible, the following procedure is recommended for in-class practice. Divide the row into two-note patterns (dyads)—the last note of each new dyad becomes the first note of the next dyad. One class member begins by singing *a* and another sings *b* and so on. The repeated note also facilitates the practice of tossing dyads.

a. Dyads

The drill can be expanded to include three-note (trichord), four-note (tetrachord), five-note (pentachord), and six-note (hexachord) patterns. This system will help you "ease" into the singing of 12-tone melodies.

b. Trichords

c. Tetrachords

d. Pentachords

e. Hexachords

As you become more proficient, it should be possible to toss patterns at random. For some extra fun in class, one class member sings the first three notes and calls the name of another who, in turn, repeats the last pitch and the next three notes. You can continue this procedure through each of the 20 melodies in section 2. In the following illustration, class members request the size of the pattern (dyad, trichord, etc.) as they are calling the student's name.

SECTION 2. Melodic Fragments: 12-Tone Series

Each of the 15 melodies represents a 12-tone series, and all are excerpted from compositions by composers such as Schoenberg, Berg, and Webern. Most have been arranged to fit within a single voice range, and many have been rewritten in a rhythmic environment more suitable to vocal music.

Preparation for this assignment began earlier with the introduction of "Twelve-Tone Models and Melodic Fragments for Interval Study."

Assuming that your expertise improved with the gradually increasing difficulty of the models and fragments in previous chapters, you should find examples of these 12-tone series well within your mastery.

SECTION 3: Creating a Coherent Melody

Using the melodies in section 2 as a guide, create a melody that uses all twelve pitches.

SECTION 4. Improvisation

Use the 12-tone series in example 11 of the previous section as the basis for improvisation.

C and D   Twentieth-Century Melodies

Among the following melodies are works by Schoenberg, Berg, Webern, Stravinsky, Anderson, and Fenner.

Berg   Violin Concerto, I (Carinthian Folk Tune)

Berg   Violin Concerto, II, from *Es ist genug!* (It Is Enough), Bach Cantata 60

Berg   Violin Concerto, II

4.

Schoenberg Chamber Symphony op. 9

5.

Webern Passacaglia op. 1

6.

Fenner "The Sprightly Companion" for Oboe and Tape, III

7.

8.

STREET SONG (Anderson) © Copyright by Bote & Bock Gmbh & Co., Berlin, a Boosey & Hawkes company. Reprinted by permission of Boosey & Hawkes, Inc.

9.

Stravinsky *Symphonies of Wind Instruments*

SYMPHONIES WIND INSTRUMENTS (Stravinsky) © Copyright 1926 by Hawkes & Son (London) Ltd. Copyright Renewed. Revised version © Copyright 1948, 1952 by Hawkes & Son (London) Ltd. Copyright Renewed. Reprinted by permission of Boosey & Hawkes, Inc.

Stravinsky *Le sacre du printemps* (The Rite of Spring)

10.

© Copyright 1921 by Edition Russe de Musique. Copyright Renewed. Copyright and Renewal assigned to Boosey & Hawkes, Inc. Reprinted by permission.

11.

Stravinsky *In Memoriam, Dylan Thomas*

Do not go gen-tle   in-to that good night,   Old age should burn and   rave   at   close of day;

Rage, rage a - gainst _ the dy   -   ing of the light . . . .

E   Ensembles of the Twentieth Century

SECTION 1.   Repertoire Using Treble and Bass Clefs

The following ensemble excerpts should be performed vocally, although instruments may be used to supplement voices. In addition to singing or playing parts in ensemble, you are encouraged to play entire excerpts at the keyboard.

In example 1 (Fenner), the special charm of "The Sprightly Companion" is found in the symmetrical patterns of a nine-note scale: 0, 1, 2, 4, 5, 6, 8, 9, 10 in an imitative texture.

1a.

Fenner   "The Sprightly Companion" for Oboe and Tape, III

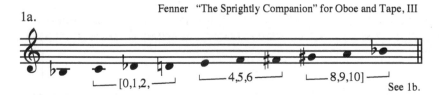

— [0,1,2,——| ——4,5,6——| ——8,9,10]——|
See 1b.

In example 2 (Schoenberg), at least three significant tetrachords are audible in the Introduction to the Variations:

Measures 4 and 7 [0,3,6,9]—"the diminished 7th tetrachord"
Measure 6 [0,2,5,7]—"the sol, la, do, re" ("I've Got Rhythm") tetrachord
Measure 7 [0,3,4,7]—"the major-minor" tetrachord, or combinations of major and minor trichords

2a.

Schoenberg *Variations for Orchestra*, op. 31

m. 4 & 7   m. 6   m. 7 (contd.)

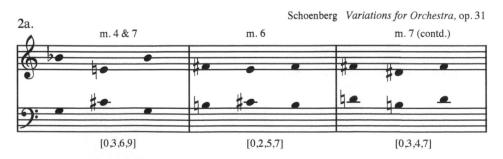

[0,3,6,9]   [0,2,5,7]   [0,3,4,7]

See 2b.

In example 3 (Schoenberg), all 12 tones are found in measures 122 and 123 (see 3b on page 326). This 12-tone piece can be used as a review of tetrachordal patterns.

Regarding example 4 (Anderson), in the composer's comment to Street Song, T. J. Anderson states: "Enculturation, the process of musically becoming, takes place for many people in children's game songs." This piece is based on a song that Mr. Anderson heard frequently while he was living in Atlanta, Georgia. The melody can be reduced to a six-note pattern:

E, D♯, E, C, A, G, C, D, C

Example 5 (Stravinsky) is taken from *Threni,* Stravinsky's first work to be written entirely in the 12-tone serial technique. Notice that the excerpt gives two forms of the series: the original and the inversion.

5a.

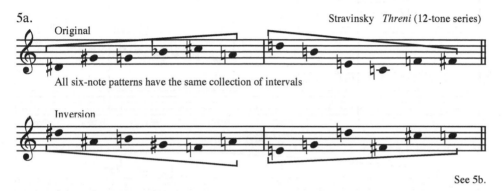

Stravinsky *Threni* (12-tone series)

THRENI (Stravinsky) © Copyright 1958 by Boosey & Co. Ltd. Copyright Renewed. Reprinted by permission of Boosey and Hawkes, Inc.

In example 6 (Stravinsky), the Carillon section of Stravinsky's *Firebird* (1910) has an elaborate atonal section, with multiple statements of a six-note pattern: [0,1,2,6,7,8] in the trumpet parts. As an experiment, students should transpose this pitch-class set at the tritone to see the order in which all six pitch classes will recur.

Stravinsky *Firebird,* R-99 (transposed to concert pitch)

6a.

[0,1,2,6,7,8]   [0,1,2,6,7,8]   [0,1,2,6,7,8]

See 6b.

In example 7 (Stravinsky), the closing measures of *Firebird* (1910) consist of a sequence of major triads in first inversion, which "harmonize" two different forms of the *Firebird* motive: [0,1,2,6].

. Stravinsky *Firebird* (closing measures)

7a.

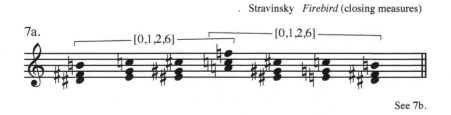

See 7b.

Fenner "The Sprightly Companion" by Burt Fenner. Reprinted by permission of D. I. Music.

It will not be necessary to transpose these instrumental parts since they are written in concert pitch.

Very quiet ♪ = 104   Schoenberg *String Trio*, op. 45

© Copyright 1950 by Boelke-Bomart, Inc., and reprinted by permission.

4b. ♩ = ca. 88   T. J. Anderson "Street Song"

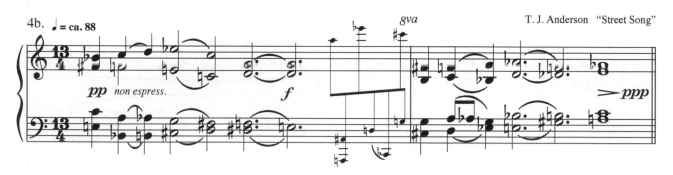

5b.   Stravinsky *Threni*

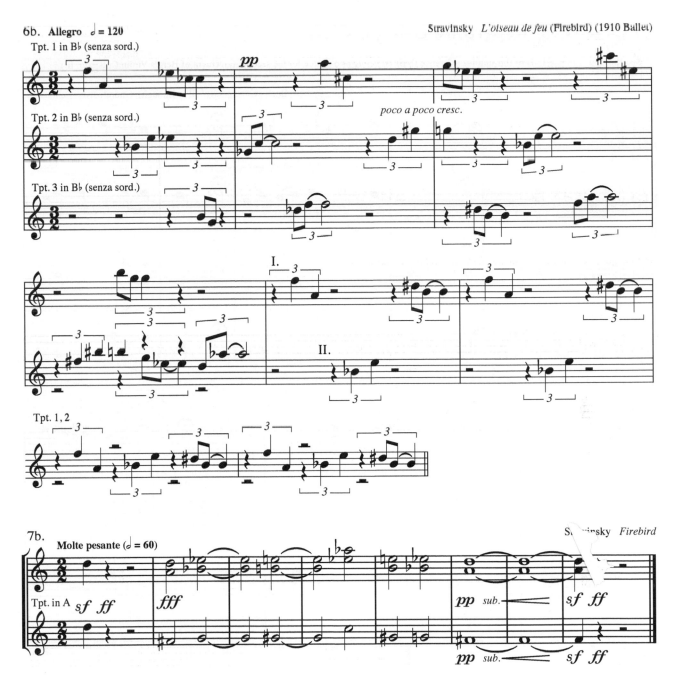

From *Firebird Ballet*, Melodies 8 & 9. Reprinted by permission of J. & W. Chester, Ltd., London.

SECTION 2. Repertoire Using C Clefs

*(See example 2 in part C-D of this unit for reference to *Es ist genug* as a source for the second movement of Berg's Violin Concerto, II.)

Bach *Es ist genug!* (It Is Enough), Chorale from Cantata 60*

1.

Holst St. Paul's Suite, "The Dargason"

(Green Sleeves)

2.

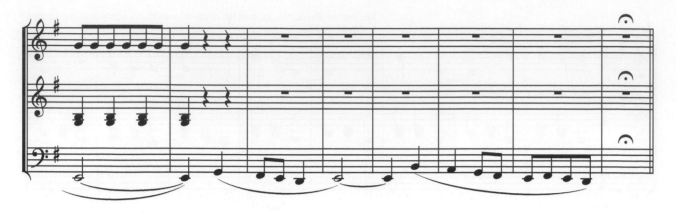

Adapted from Berlin, Editions Russes de Musique, n.d. (1912). Reprinted: Dover Editions, 1988.

Composer and Genre Index

American
    "Come, Thou Fount of Every Blessing," 50
    "Driving Saw-Logs on the Plover," 142
    "How We Got Up to the Woods Last Year," 103
    "I Am a River Driver," 103
    "King and Queen," 44
    "Old Joe Clark," 202
    "The Raftsmen's Song," 104
    "Save Your Money While You're Young," 143
Appalachian, "Barbara Ellen," 226
Bulgarian, Folk song, 229
Creek Ceremonial Song, "Skeleton Dance," 62
Creole (Louisiana)
    "Aine, dé, trois, Caroline," 83
    "Aurore Pradère," 82
    "Belle Layotte," 82–83
    "Dialogue d' Amour," 84
    "Quand mo-té jeune," 83
English sea shanty, "Drunken Sailor," 201
French-Canadian, "La Bastringue," 44
Greek, Folk Song, 279
Haitian
    "Fai Ogoun," 143
    "Ma frê," 143
Jamaican
    "Back to the Tropics," 61
    "Banana Boat Song," 45
    "Big, Big Sambo Gal," 69
    "Cudelia Brown," 88
    "Mattie Rag," 61, 80
    "Mattie walla lef," 80
    "Ratta Madan Law," 61
Jewish lullaby, "Lulla, Lulla," 202–203
Russian, "My Sweetheart," 228
Spanish, "Navalafuente," 230
Switzerland, "Z' Basel an mym Rhy," 104
Fossa, Johann de, *Litany of the Blessed Virgin Mary, Kyrie; Christe,* 110–112
Franck, César, *Violin Sonata,* II, 179
French children's song, "Ah, vous dirai-je, Maman," 7
Fux, Johann Joseph, *Serie VII—Theoretische und pädigogische Werke* from *Samtliche Werke*
    #17, 16, 17
    #27, 35
    #28, 35

G

Gabrieli, Andrea
    "A caso un giorno," 85
    "Che giova posseder," 88–91
Glocke, Dennis, conducting patterns, 1, 18, 175
Graaf, Charles E., Mozart adaptation of, 7
Grainger, Percy
    Colonial Song, 80
    Irish Tune from County Derry, 80
Gregorian Chant. *See also* Hildegard von Bingen
    Dies Irae, 225
    Hymn to St. Thomas Aquinas, 205
    In Paradisum, 206
    Kyrie IX (Cum jubilo), 49
    Kyrie XI (Orbis factor), 48
    Kyrie eleison—Requiem Mass, 6
    Sanctus IX (Cum jubilo), 49
    Veni Sancte Spiritus—Pentecost (abridged), 6

Griffes, Charles T., *Symphony in Yellow* (op. 3, no. 2), 298–299

H

Händel, Georg Friedrich
    Julius Caesar, act I, 140
    Suite no. 1, *Menuet* (HWV 434), 126
    Suite no. 3, var. 4 (HWV 428), 126
    Suite no. 4, *Sarabande,* var. 1 (HWV 437), 127
    Suite no. 5, *Air* ("The Harmonious Blacksmith") (HWV 430), 127
    Suite no. 7, *Gigue* (HWV 440), 125
    Suite no. 8, *Gigue* (HWV 441), 126
    Suite no. 9 (HWV 442)
        Chaconne, 126
        var. 62, 127
    Wassermusik
        Suite no. 1 (HWV 348, 4, 8), 125
        Suite no. 2 (HWV 349, 12), 125
Haydn, Franz Joseph
    Allegro molto in D Major (fragment), 28
    Capriccio (Hob. XVII:1), 28
    Das strickende Mädchen, 249
    Die Heiligen Zehn Gebote als Canons (no. 8), "Achtes Gebote," 168–169
    Die Zehn Gebote der Kunst (no. 1), 128
    Dir nah ich mich, nah mich dem Throne, 198
    Gott im Herzen, 145–146
    Hob. XVI:3, 28
    Hob. XVI:12, III, 28
    Minuet in G Major (Hob. XVI:11), III, 28
    Nine Early Sonatas, no. 9, III, 28
    Piano Sonatas
        (Hob. XVI:5), Trio, 250
        (Hob. XVI:12), II, 198
        (Hob. XVI:16), II, 198
    Sonata in D Major (Hob. XVI:51), II, 28
    String Quartets
        (op. 17, no. 5, II, Minuet and Trio), 70–73
        (op. 74, no. 3, I), 250
        (op. 76, no. 4, I,), 249
    Symphonies
        "Drumroll" (op. 103)
            II, 73
            III, 74
        no. 88, II, 120
        no. 94
            II, 40, 120
            III, 40
    Thy Voice O Harmony, 190
    Variations (Hob. XVII:2) (vars. 2, 16), 28
    Variations (Hob. XVII:5) (theme), 28
Hebrew songs. *See also* Folk Songs, Jewish; Songs of the Babylonian Jews
    "Adon Olam," 62
    "Ets Chayim Hi," 64
    "Hevenu Shalom Aleychem," 62
    "Hin'ni Muchan Um'zuman," 62
    "L'cha Dodi," 63
    "Sim Shalom," 64
    "Yigdal," 63
    "Yismach Moshe," 63
Hensel, Fanny Mendelssohn, *Schwanenlied,* 237